THE LIFE OF JESUS CHRIST
Fenceposts IV

Mike Woodruff
SENIOR PASTOR, CHRIST CHURCH

100 N Waukegan Rd
Lake Forest, Illinois 60045
847-234-1001
www.christchurchil.org

TABLE OF CONTENTS

PREFACE

Three thousand years ago, King Solomon lamented, "of the writing of many books there is no end." Had he lived today he might have said the same thing regarding books about Jesus. After all, a new one comes out almost every week – forty to fifty every year. It's likely that there are enough books about Jesus to fill a Barnes and Noble, perhaps several of them.

Stop and think about that for a moment. Most people's influence begins to wane the moment they die. Not Jesus. He has been gaining momentum for the last two thousand years. Amazing.

Of course, the fact that there are already hundreds of thousands (millions?) of books about Christ begs the question, "Why write another one?" Do I have anything to say about Jesus that hasn't already been said several thousand times before? Probably not. But here's why I decided to write this one anyway.

First, I wrote it because you were likely to read it. The chances are high that this book found its way into your hand because you know me – or you know someone who knows me. I didn't write it to land on a best-seller list. I'm writing as a pastor and a friend trying to push people I know and love closer to God. A few years ago I became persuaded that this was one way I could do that – i.e., if I wrote a book about Jesus many people I know would read it. And since you are reading this page, you might say I wrote this book just for you.

Second, I wrote this book for me. I didn't realize this was what I was doing when I set out, but I'm now convinced that it was the plan behind the plan. I learn by writing, and I wanted (and want) to learn more about God. And on top of this it was both fun and fascinating. What better topic to take on than the most interesting, influential and fascinating person who ever lived. As I have shared with several friends, I've been reading and studying the Gospels for thirty years. You would think that by now I would have learned everything there is to know about Jesus. In fact, you'd think the writings of Matthew, Mark, Luke and John might be growing stale for me. But the opposite is true; the more I study the more I realize just how infinitely amazing Jesus is.

Finally, this work is a critical addition to an ongoing series. A few years ago

I began The FencePosts Project. The idea behind the metaphor is that, while it's not necessary for Christ followers to believe the same thing about every single aspect of the Christian faith, there are a handful of foundational truths that serve as fence posts – markers indicating the dividing line between what is acceptable and what is not. When you connect these posts together they form a protected zone. Everything inside is safe. This book is the fourth in a series of five studies. They loosely correspond to the tenets of faith found at Christ Church.

As with most writing projects, this was a team effort. Indeed, I was offered more encouragement and editing than I deserve. Those who helped know where they are. I am not going to start naming them, both for fear of leaving out a critical few, and also for fear of sharing the blame. The mistakes are mine; hopefully they are few.

May this work will help you move closer to Christ!

Soli Deo Gloria

Mike Woodruff

CHAPTER 1:
LOOK AGAIN

I know men and I tell you that Jesus Christ is no mere man. Between him and every other person in the world there is no possible terms of comparison. Alexander, Caesar, Charlemagne and I have founded empires. But on what did we rest the creation of our glories? Upon force. Jesus Christ founded His empire on love, and at this hour millions of men would die for him.
Napoleon Bonaparte

Either this man was, and is, the Son of God; or else a madman or something worse. You can shut him up for a fool, you can spit at him and kill him as a demon, or you can fall at his feet and call him Lord and God. But let us not come up with any patronizing nonsense about his being a great moral teacher. He has not left that door open to us. He did not intend to.
C.S. Lewis

What is beyond dispute is that Jesus of Nazareth is one of those perennial question marks in history with which mankind is never quite done. With a ministry of two or three years he attracted and infuriated his contemporaries, mesmerized and alienated the ancient world, unleashed a movement that has done the same ever since, and thus changed the course of history forever.
J.P. Meier

I'd like you to take another look at Jesus.

I say "another" because I'm pretty sure you already have an opinion. You know something about him. It's hard not to. After all, he is one of the most revered and reviled people of all time.

My request is that you take another look at Jesus. Whether you exalt him as God, write him off as a deluded mystic or place him at one of the many points in between, I ask that you review his claims, teachings and example in light of the New Testament documents and the latest insights from historians.

There are at least seven reasons to do so.

Reason One: He is the most influential person who ever lived

No one has affected the world more than this first-century carpenter. No one. It is an accomplishment made all the more stunning given the obstacles he had to overcome. Here was a man who was born two thousand years ago to a young peasant girl in an obscure village in the backwaters of the Roman Empire. He worked as a carpenter until he was thirty and died on a cross between two thieves before turning thirty-four. He never wrote a book, held office, owned a home or attended college. He never traveled more than 200 miles from the place he was born. In fact, he did not do any of the things that usually accompany greatness. He should have been forgotten. And yet, two thousand years later his influence is unmatched and it continues to grow.

Consider a few of the items he could list on his resume:

- More books have been written about him than have been written about any other person who ever lived. [1]
- He has inspired more paintings and music than anyone else.
- Tens of thousands of schools, colleges, hospitals, orphanages and homeless shelters have been founded in his honor.
- His followers credit him with their efforts to abolish slavery, educate the masses and end poverty.
- His birthday is the largest annual celebration in the world.
- Millions of people have laid down their lives for him, and millions more stand ready to do so.
- His followers currently number close to two billion.

And perhaps the most stunning accomplishment of all: millions of people are studying his life and teachings at this very moment. They do so in hopes of becoming more like him. [2]

Sixty billion people have walked on this planet.[3] Most have left it unchanged. Very few have made a lasting mark. Jesus fundamentally reshaped it. More than any person in history, this carpenter from Nazareth has formed our world. Every educated person should know why.

Reason Two: He is the greatest teacher who ever lived.

Assessing a teacher's performance is complicated. It follows that declaring someone to be "the greatest teacher to ever live" will be controversial. But there are a handful of reasons to think that Christ is just that.

- **He gave us the greatest ethical system we have.** Before Christ told us to "love our enemies," "turn the other cheek," and "do to others what you'd want them to do to you," most people's idea of the high road was limiting revenge to an "eye for an eye and a tooth for a tooth."[4] Jesus changed that. He turned the world upside down by arguing that those "who want to be great must be a servant," and that only those "who are without sin should cast the first stone." Professional philosophers may debate whether Aristotle's Nicomedian Ethics or Christ's Sermon on the Mount stands as the greatest ethical system. Moral reformers do not. Mahatma Ghandi, Martin Luther King, Mother Theresa and hundreds of others all point to Christ.

- **He was a master of the craft.** Set aside the content of Christ's teaching, his mastery of parables, ability to turn everyday events into spiritual lessons and his practice of answering the question behind the question are enough to qualify him for the Teacher's Hall of Fame. If you need convincing, grab a red letter Bible and read the black letters that follow the red ones. What you find among those who have met with Christ is that they are struggling to regain their balance. Jesus has left them stunned. When they finally speak, it's generally to say something like, "We've never heard any of this before." Or "No one has ever spoken to us with this authority before."[5]

- **His action matched his words.** Christ not only called others to live simply, he did so himself. He not only taught that the way to be great was to serve, he washed his disciples' feet. Those in power often claim exemptions from following the rules they impose upon others. Jesus did not. There was no daylight between what he taught and what he did.

- **His legacy is unmatched.** Finally, there is no denying that Jesus turned a group of uneducated and unimpressive "also-rans" into an unstoppable platoon of disciples. In fact, those he left behind launched the largest and longest-lasting ideological revolution in the history of the world. Does anyone believe Peter, James or John would have done that if they had not been coached by Jesus?

Reason Three: He claimed to be God.

The same person who made the most profound impact on humanity and who deserves the title "Greatest Teacher of All Time" also made the most outlandish claim possible: He said he was God.

No greater claim can be made.

Sure, others have made it; David Koresh of Waco and Jim Jones from Guyana are two examples. But few believed them then and no one believes them now. Christ impacted thousands during his life and billions since. Or, to state this differently, while anyone can claim to be God, and some others do, no one of Jesus' stature does. He is the only great moral leader to ever make this claim.

As C.S. Lewis writes:

> There is no parallel in other religions. If you had gone to Buddha and asked him: "Are you the son of Brahma?" he would have said, "My Son, you are still in the veil of illusion." If you had gone to Socrates and asked, "Are you Zeus?" he would have laughed at you. If you had gone to Mohammed and asked, "Are you Allah?" he would first have rent his clothes and then cut your head off. If you had asked Confucius, "Are you Heaven?" I think he would have probably replied, "Remarks which are not in accordance with nature are in bad taste." The idea of a great moral teacher saying what Christ said is out of the question. In my opinion, the only person who can say that sort of thing is either God or a complete lunatic suffering from that form of delusion which undermines the whole mind of man.[6]

Think about this. A man who otherwise demonstrated remarkable humility:[7]

- Said that he and the Father were One.

- Used the titles of God to refer to himself.
- Accepted worship, forgave sins and acted in other ways that only God should act.
- Claimed that he would return at the end of the age to judge every person who ever lived.[8]

Can you imagine bolder claims?

Others have claimed to speak for God. But Jesus went further. He claimed to be God. Not godly. Not god-like. Not even "a god." Jesus claimed to be the one true God.

Reason Four: You likely know less about this than you think

It's always risky to generalize, and you may be the clear exception. But I have a couple reasons to think that you may know less about Christ and the revolution he launched than you think.

My Experience: For starters, there is my own background. The Jesus I was introduced to in my kindergarten Sunday school class was as thin as the flannel graph piece of cloth used to represent him. I cannot claim to remember the specifics, but I can say that my take-away was a first century version of Mr. Rogers – the kind of perennial goody-goody you might get if you mixed Snow White with an Eagle Scout. He was always smiling, never raised his voice and was kind to children and small forest animals.

The problem is, this is not the Jesus of the New Testament. There is no way to reconcile my understanding of Christ with the man who threw the money changers out of the temple, called the religious leaders "unwashed graves" and profoundly unnerved Pilate.

My Observation: The first reason I think many people know less about Jesus is because I held onto my kindergarten image through high school. The second reason is because I've listened to the Jesus other people say they believe in, and my take is that he generally looks a lot like they do, only he's a bit nicer.

Republicans act like Jesus founded the NRA. Liberals' claim he crusaded for labor unions, and socialists maintain he dressed like Che Guevara.[9] During the last thirty years I've seen Christ claimed by virtually every side of every issue: Jesus the capitalist and Jesus the Marxist; Jesus the pacifist and Jesus the warrior; Jesus the environmentalist and Jesus the corporate titan. Some of this is simple opportunism. (You could do worse than recruit Jesus as a spokesman.) But many people invoke his name based on a misunderstanding of his life, teaching and central message. Few of us understand him as well as we think.[10]

Many people end up making Jesus a lot like themselves, only nicer.

Reason Five: There are good reasons to believe that he is God

I should start by noting that we cannot prove this point. At least not in the way that the word "prove" is generally used today. Since the Enlightenment we want facts, and we want them delivered by people wearing white lab coats. But Christianity is not a scientific claim, it's an historical one. And you can't prove history in a lab. We cannot rewind events and replay them over and over, controlling for different variables until we definitively prove the hypothesis true or false.

Historians base their beliefs on reports of events. They interview first and second hand witnesses – or read their accounts – and then offer their understanding of what actually happened.
The Christian faith rests on such evidence.[11] In his first letter to the church in Corinth, the Apostle Paul writes:

> For what I received I passed on to you as of first importance:
> that Christ died for our sins according to the Scriptures, that he
> was buried, that he was raised on the third day according to the
> Scriptures, and that he appeared to Cephas, and then to the Twelve.
> After that, he appeared to more than five hundred of the brothers
> and sisters at the same time, most of whom are still living, though
> some have fallen asleep. Then he appeared to James, then to all the
> apostles, and last of all he appeared to me also, as to one abnormally
> born.[12]

Paul grounds the Christian faith on the testimony of over five hundred witnesses. He does not suggest that we should have faith without evidence, or believe in Christ "because Christianity works" or "will make us feel better." He argues that we should believe that Jesus Christ is the promised Savior of the World because the resurrection actually happened - Jesus rose from the dead just as he claimed he would.

A Brief Time Out

Christianity is not a small topic. In fact, it claims to be the way we are to understand everything. It follows that it's hard to explain it without occasionally backing up to explain a piece of it. At this moment I need to call a time out and explain two things: the basic tenets of the Christian faith and the way we understand the miraculous claims found in the New Testament.

The Tenets of the Christian Faith: Christianity revolves around Christ. In fact, while you could have Buddhism without Buddha, Judaism without Moses and Islam without Mohammed, you could not have Christianity without Christ.

But the claims of Christ are not limited to his life. The Christian faith is a way of understanding everything, and the basic tenets reach beyond Christ. While I am not going to set every tenet before you, I believe there are a handful of the most basic that you need to hear.

- Jesus Christ is God.

- Jesus Christ existed from before time began. In fact, he was there when the universe was made.

- At the incarnation, Christ became man. That is, while remaining fully God he became fully man. He did this in order to rescue us from sin and death. By dying in our place he paid our moral debt. This allows those who accept his payment to be reconciled with God.

- The Old Testament (Hebrew Scriptures) is about Christ. After opening with a brief explanation of our situation – i.e., we were made in

God's image but became estranged from God because of sin – God promises to send a rescuer. In Genesis 12 he calls Abraham to be the father of the people through whom the Savior will be born. Beginning with this "call" in Genesis 12, the entire Old Testament is a run-up to Christ's birth.

- The Gospels – i.e., Matthew, Mark, Luke and John – tell the story of Christ's life. They begin with the announcement of his virgin conception, briefly cover his birth and early years, and then focus almost exclusively on his death and resurrection.

- Christ's death and resurrection are understood to be the focal point of history. In fact, the resurrection is offered as proof that he is who he claimed to be. The New Testament documents contend that if the resurrection did not happen then Christianity is not true. But if it did happen then it is. If Christ rose from the dead he is most certainly who he claimed to be: God himself and the Savior of the world.

- The rest of the New Testament – i.e., the story of the first thirty years of the church (the Acts of the Apostles), the letters written by the apostles[13] and the final "look ahead" (the Book of Revelation) – were written to help us better understand Christ's life and mission. They are critical because it's not always enough to know what happened; we also need to know something of the event's significance. For instance, being told that a group of men crossed a small river in a row boat could mean a variety of things. If the river was the Rubicon, the men were being led by Julius Caesar and in crossing it he was declaring war on Pompey, we need to be told that. Similarly, there is a big difference between "Christ died" and "Christ died for our sins." The first is a simple matter of history. The second is an explanation of the Christian faith.[14]

The Miracles of Christ: The New Testament is the most remarkably and rigorously attested ancient document in existence. The number, date and quality of the ancient manuscripts is astounding. And the story it reports is supported by first and second century non-Christian historians.

In fact, even though first-century Palestine lacked today's international news media, and in spite of the fact that most of what was written back then has been lost, there is enough historical information outside of the New Testament to establish that:

- A person named Jesus lived in the first century region of Judea.

- He was a provocative teacher and a wise and virtuous man.

- He reportedly performed miracles and made prophetic claims.

- The Jewish leaders condemned him for acts of sorcery and apostasy.

- He was crucified by the Roman procurator Pontius Pilate at the time of the Jewish Passover during the reign of the Emperor Tiberius.

- Christ's followers - called Christians - reported that he had risen from the dead.

- This launched the Christian faith, which quickly spread to Rome and beyond, even though Christians were persecuted and martyred for their faith.

- First-century Christians worshiped Jesus Christ as God and celebrated the Lord's Supper in their services. While at times the Romans ridiculed the followers of Christ as morally weak, these disciples were often known for their courage and virtue.

Considering that most ancient historians focused on political and military leaders, not on obscure rabbis from the outskirts of the Roman Empire, this is remarkable information. What it means is that Jewish, Greek and Roman historians confirm the major events that are presented in the New Testament.

Nevertheless, the primary source that Christians turn to are those found in the New Testament. But, because the New Testament books contain reports of miracles – e.g., Christ healing the sick, calming a storm and raising the dead – many believe that they cannot be trusted. A full defense of miracles (let alone the New Testament) is outside the scope of this essay, but I do want to briefly acknowledge the skepticism and speak directly to it.[15]

Several things are worth noting:

- **The Gospels do not read like myth.** Matthew, Mark, Luke and John claim to be first- and second-hand accounts of the life of Jesus, and that is how they come across. Yes, they report supernatural events, but they do so without sounding like Aesop's Fables. Instead of beginning "a long time ago in a far away land," they are carefully set in the context of precise historical references. Dates, geographical settings and the names of contemporary politicians are all noted.[16]

- **The miracles are central to the story.** There are not as many miracles in the New Testament as many people think, but those that are reported drive much of the story.[17] Consequently, if you take them out – e.g., if you argue that Jesus did not calm a storm, he simply predicted the weather, or he did not walk on water, he simply found a sand bar[18] – you end up with several problems. First, some of what he taught was based on the miracles he performed. Take away the miracle and you have to give up the teaching. Second, much of what he taught was about himself – specifically, it focused on his claim to be God. If you take all of this away there is not much left.[19] Finally, if you take away the miracles you cannot explain his popularity. Jesus drew large crowds just about everywhere he went. Are we to believe people followed him all over Palestine just to hear him say, "be nice?"

- **It would be odd if Christ did not reveal his power.** Can you imagine what the skeptics would say if Christ claimed to be God but never revealed any unique powers? They would demand proof. The problem is, once "proof" is offered it is discounted. In fact, the proof is used to discredit the entire story. A thoughtful reading of the Gospels actually presents quite a balanced report. Unlike the faith healers of his day (or ours), Christ did not create a circus-like atmosphere or brag about his abilities. Instead, he quietly met the needs of troubled people by exercising the same kind of authority over sickness, evil and nature that he did over people.[20] How would you expect God-in-the-flesh to act?

- **The disciples were utterly convinced that He had risen from the dead.** Critics of Christianity either portray the disciples as simpletons who were easily misled by third-rate magic or as conniving schemers who pulled off the biggest hoax in history. Neither conclusion is supported by the facts. Far from being quickly persuaded that Jesus was God, the disciples seem to take forever to get it. But once they did "get it" they were unshakable. Ten of the twelve die as martyrs for their faith. Whether Jesus was God or not, it is clear that they believed he was.

- **The disciples were among the people least likely to believe that Jesus was God.** All twelve of the apostles were Jews, which meant two things: they believed in one God, and they believed that this God was infinite, holy and transcendent – i.e., he could be walking around next to them. In order to be persuaded that Jesus was God-incarnate these men had to modify just about all of their most-deeply-held beliefs – and they did.[21]

- **Jesus perfectly fulfilled the Hebrew prophecies.** The Hebrew Scriptures contains several hundred descriptions about the Jewish Messiah. All of these were written at least four hundred years before Christ was born. Many lay beyond his ability to influence – and yet he perfectly fulfilled them. The odds of this happening are beyond astronomical.

- **Even his critics conceded his exceptional abilities.** Historians pay special attention to the writings of critics, believing that any point that a critic concedes against their case is almost certainly true. In the case of Christ, the critics concede that he has some sort of supernatural power. They attribute it to the devil, not to God, but they are forced to admit that he possesses unique powers.[22]

Your skepticism is likely shaped more by your starting assumptions than by the evidence itself – and that is not the way it is supposed to work. In fact, it's a bit irrational. Christianity rests on a historical claim. You owe it to yourself to consider the historical evidence.

Reason Six: He is Not Just a Good Person

Many people contend that Jesus is the one thing he could not possibly be - a good man but nothing more. They applaud his ethics and example, celebrate his selflessness, and suggest that he was both a wise sage and a gifted spiritual guide. In short, they affirm him in every way possible except in his central claim: that he is God. And yet, if Jesus is not who he claimed to be, then the one thing he could not be is a good man. Because he either knew he was not god and lied about it, or he thought he was god but was deluded.

If I tell you that I am a fifty year old, happily married father of three with a bad golf swing, you'll probably think, "That sounds about right." If I go on to say that, "I'm better looking than anyone else you've met," you'll either think I'm making a joke or hopelessly vain. If I go further – e.g., if I claim that I am smarter than Einstein and can run faster than any Olympic athlete, you'll begin to think that I'm delusional and need help.[23] But if I claim to be God Almighty – the creator of heaven and earth, the judge of all humanity, the Bread of Life and Light of the World and that you should reorder your life to revolve around me – you would think that I had completely lost my mind.

Jesus made all of those claims and more. If they are not true, he is not a good person. He is either a liar or a narcissist. The early church understood this, which is why one of their earliest statements about Christ was: aut Deus aut homo malus – Jesus is either 'God or a bad man.'

Reason Seven: The Stakes are High

The final reason I think you should take another look at Christ is because the stakes are so high.

A few years ago I stopped by my doctor's office to be vaccinated before traveling to a meeting in Africa. Together we consulted the Center for Disease Control's guidelines for the area I was going to be visiting. After thinking for a few minutes my doctor said, "Four shots are listed. Three of them are no brainers. You have to have them. But there is one shot you need to think about. The odds that you'll contract this disease are low. And the shot is very expensive. But, if you catch this disease you will really regret not getting this shot. First you'll get very sick, then you'll wish you'd die, and then you will."

In other words, the risks were low but the stakes were high.

When it comes to Jesus I'm convinced that both the risks and stakes are high. That is, I believe that the chances are really good that Jesus is who he claims to be. And I think that any stakes that involve our eternal destiny – which is what Christ says is in play – are high by definition.

Conclusion

If I thought I could hold your attention much longer I'd keep listing reasons why you should take another look at Jesus - such as my conviction that he is the most attractive personality you'll ever meet and my belief that he is the answer to the deepest longings you have. But I've had my chance. I've listed seven reasons to take another look at Christ. I now invite you to do just that.

In the five chapters that follow we are going to unpack the life of Jesus. We'll start by tracing the biblical account of his life and work through a variety of different stages, beginning before creation and moving through his birth, childhood and public ministry and continuing all the way through what we are told about his death, resurrection, ascension and exaltation. We will then end with a chapter devoted to examining the most commonly asked questions people have about Jesus.

ENDNOTES

[1] The Gospels have been translated into more languages than anything else ever written, and numerous people devote decades of their life to learn languages with the expressed purpose of translating the New Testament into that language.

[2] There are several points worth noting here: 1) Christianity is the fastest growing religion in the world; 2) it is growing rapidly through conversion; and 3) because of this more books have been written about Christ in the last twenty years than in the previous 1,900.

[3] John Blanchard, Why on Earth Did Jesus Come (EP Books, 2009).

[4] Never mind that this approach would leave most of us blind, it was a step down from revenge.

[5] I made a decision to become a Christ follower more than 30 years ago. Since that time I have been studying his life and teachings on an almost daily basis. In preparation for this book I spent ten weeks focused almost exclusively on his life and work. Two things struck me about that experience: 1) How much I didn't know. Jesus struck me as a source of infinite wisdom and truth – a well that would never run dry. (John writes at the end of his Gospel, "If everything Jesus did was written down the whole world wouldn't

have room for the books that would be needed.") and 2) How fresh his words and story remain. It does not grow old. This is equally shocking. Who can sustain this level of inquiry? Whose words can remain powerful and shocking when you read them for the two-hundredth time?

[6] C.S. Lewis, "What Are We to Make of Jesus Christ?" (1950)

[7] I occasionally meet people who argue that Jesus did not actually claim to be God. We will explain the many ways he did so. At this moment I will only note that those who heard him speak accused him of blasphemy. Indeed, this is the main reason that religious leaders wanted Christ put to death.

[8] Christ claimed that at the end of "the age" he will return as King, and that in that role he will judge everyone who has ever lived. He further claims that his assessment will be both perfect and final, and that it will be based in large part on how people responded to him.

[9] Mikhail Gorbachev said, "Jesus was the first socialist. The first to seek a better life for mankind."

[10] As Michael Massing said, "Many who like Jesus have found him exactly what they like." Michael Massing, America's Favorite Philosopher, The New York Times Book Review, Dec. 28th, 2003, p. 7. For the record, it is not only true that people assume that Jesus thinks the way they think, it is also true that many assume that Jesus looks like they look – e.g., in spite of the fact that he was a first century Jew, most citizens of the U.S. picture him as an handsome Anglo with blue eyes and white teeth.

[11] It is important to note that the Christian faith is based on historic claims. I highlight this because some mistakenly believe it is based on a "faith claim" – i.e., it is based entirely on wishful thinking – and others view it as an ethical system or a philosophical argument, both of which are based on reason.

[12] I Cor. 15:3ff

[13] The New Testament letters – which are occasionally called Epistles – were written by Paul, Peter, James and John, all of whom are identified as apostles. The writer of the Letter to the Hebrews is not identified. Some scholars think it was Paul; others do not. It is possible that it was written by someone other than an apostle.

[14] In his book Understanding Jesus, Alister McGrath develops this point in greater detail. The example he uses is of Julius Caesar crossing a small river with a single legion of men in 49 B.C. The name of the river was the

Rubicon, and it marked the boundary between Italy and Cisalpine Gual. The event was the simple crossing of the river. The significance of the event was that it marked a declaration of war by Caesar against Pompey. In a similar way, the Christian faith is based upon certain historical events – but it is not identified by these events alone. These events need to be interpreted. In many cases the Gospels interpret themselves. However, it is not unusual for the event to only be fully understood: 1) later, after other events; 2) in light of an earlier prophecy; or 3) after additional information has been shared in one of the letters that make up the New Testament. In this study I will be doing my best to indicate the significance behind many of the major events that are being reported. (Alister McGrath, Understanding Jesus, Zondervan, 1987, p. 23.

[15] As noted earlier, I am basing the exploration of the life of Christ on the Gospels because they are the best source of information we have on his life. In chapter seven I will address the question of their reliability in greater length. At this point let me simply note that the history reported in the Gospels has been corroborated by outside sources. You do not have to believe that they are inspired by God to acknowledge the degree to which they have been validated. Luke in particular is singled out as a first rate historian. Dr. John McRay, a professor of New Testament and Archeology at Wheaton College, speaks for many when he writes, "The general consensus of both liberal and conservative scholars is that Luke is very accurate as a historian. He's erudite, he's eloquent, his Greek approaches classical quality, he writes as an educated man, and archeological discoveries are showing over and over again that Luke is accurate in what he has to say." John McRay, quoted by Lee Strobel, The Case for Christ, Grand Rapids: Zondervan, 1998, p. 129.

[16] C.S. Lewis's comments here are especially helpful. Lewis wrote The Chronicles of Narnia – one of the most successful myths of the twentieth century. He was also a professor of Medieval Literature at both Oxford and Cambridge Universities – and in that capacity was an expert on myths. He writes: "Turn to John. Read the dialogues: that with the Samaritan women at the well, or that which follows the healing of the man born blind…I have been reading poems, romances, vision-literature, legends and myths all my life. I know what they are like. Of this text there are only two possible views. Either this is reportage…pretty close to the facts…Or else, some unknown writer in the second century, without known predecessors or successors, suddenly anticipated the whole technique of modern, novelistic, realistic narrative. If it is untrue, it must be narrative of that kind. The reader who doesn't see this has simply not learned to read." C.S. Lewis, Fern-seed and Elephants, p. 108, cited by J.I. Packer, Celebrating the Saving Work of God (Paternoster Press, 1998), p. 30.

[17] In his book, The Jesus I Never Knew, Philip Yancey argues that once you accept the idea that Christ is God, the question is not, "Why did he do so

many miracles," but "Why did he do so few?"

[18] Likewise, he didn't feed 5000 (plus women and children) – that number was inflated, or, the "real miracle" was the example of the boy who went first. After he shared his lunch everyone else saw the value of sharing and brought out the food they had brought.

[19] As we will see later on, Christ's teaching is principally about himself. To be more direct, it is principally about the fact that he is the Son of God. After you take those sections out and those sections that follow or set up a miracle, there is not much left.

[20] If you study the miracles of Christ a few things become clear: 1) They fell loosely into three categories: healings, power over nature (silencing a storm, turning water into wine, etc.), and exorcisms; 2) It was as a healer that Jesus was famous. (There are twenty specific accounts of healings – including raising the dead – plus several general statements about the large number of people healed by Christ. Mk. 1:32-34; 3:7-12; 6:55f; Lk 7:21f). There are not that many other miracles: eight displays of power over nature and six exorcisms. When you step back and consider these miracles more broadly, you realize how perfectly they compliment his life and claims. His exorcisms displayed his power over evil. The feeding of 5,000 not only set up his claim to be the "Bread of Life" but also shows his power over nature. He changed the water intended to be used to keep people ceremonially clean and turned it into wine. (PB 112)

[21] Every day the Jews would recite the Shema: "Hear O Israel, the Lord our God, the Lord is One." Believing that God was one while believing that God the Father was God and that Jesus Christ was God – and doing so before any concept of the Trinity had come into view – meant that Jesus could not be God. And yet Jesus was so clearly God that they began to worship him as just that.

[22] Celsus, a Greek critic, stated that Christ "practiced magic." (Origen, Contra Celsum 1.38). The arrest warrant issued by the Jewish leaders (Sanhedrin 43a) reported that, "Yeshua of Nazareth" was to be stoned "because he practiced sorcery."(Note: Jesus was not stoned, he was crucified. However, this warrant was issued by Jewish authorities not Roman ones. If the Jews had put Christ to death it would have been by stoning.) The critical point is that both accounts acknowledge that Jesus had special powers.

[23] Psychologists tell us that one of the ways to assess our mental health is to measure the distance between 'who we think we are' and 'who we actually are.'

CHAPTER 2
Emmanuel – God with Us
From Before Time Began
to God With Us

God slipped into human nature like someone putting on dungarees in order to repair the world after a breakdown.
Walter Kasper

The Omnipotent, in one instant, made himself breakable. He who had been spirit became pierceable. He who was larger than the universe became an embryo. And he who sustains the world with a word chose to be dependent upon the nourishment of a young girl. God as a fetus. Holiness sleeping in a womb. The creator of life being created. God was given eyebrows, elbows, two kidneys, and a spleen. He stretched against the walls and floated in the amniotic fluids of his mother.
Max Lucado

Veiled in flesh the Godhead see, Hail the incarnate Deity,
Pleased as man with men to dwell, Jesus our Emmanuel.
Charles Wesley

It's usually best to start at the beginning. Unfortunately, when it comes to Jesus, few back up far enough to do that. It's an honest mistake. After all, most people equate his beginning with his birth, and they know the story of his birth quite well. It's hard not to. Every December the second chapter of Luke turns up everywhere, including The Charlie Brown Christmas Special, where Linus quotes it at length:

In those days Caesar Augustus issued a decree that a census should be taken of the entire Roman world. So Joseph went up from the town of Nazareth in Galilee to Judea, to Bethlehem the town of David, because he belonged to the house and line of David. He went there to register with Mary, who was pledged to be married to him and was expecting a child.

But Christ's story does not begin with his birth. It begins long before that. And if we have any hope of understanding who he is, we need to read his story in its full context. That requires beginning before time began and proceeding forward from there.

In this chapter we will do just that. We'll back up to the very beginning, consider what the Bible has to say about Christ in the "land before time," make some additional observations about his role during the Old Testament

Before Time

Carl Sagan famously stated, "The cosmos is all that is, or ever was or ever will be." Those who embrace this worldview do not believe that anything existed before the universe was formed.

The Bible contends that God did.   More to the point, the Bible contends that Jesus did.   Alongside the Father and the Spirit, the Son of God existed before time in his pre-incarnate (pre-human-body) state. This means that Jesus not only existed as a divine being before he was born, it means that he existed before anything else did.[1]

The Apostle John opens with this claim. In the very first line of his Gospel he writes:

> In the beginning was the Word and the Word was with God and the Word was God. He was with God in the beginning. Through him all things were made; without him nothing was made that has been made.

The term translated Word in our English Bible is the Greek word logos. Ancient Greek philosophers used it to refer to a principle of order and knowledge, a word or discourse. John borrows it to refer to Jesus Christ before he was born. He asserts that the Word (Jesus) existed as God before the universe was formed.[2]

This is a huge claim.

It means that Jesus is profoundly different from you and me, and that his birth was different from yours and mine. We came into being at the time of our conception. Jesus existed before his. Mary's pregnancy did not mark the start of his life, just the start of his life as a man. He had existed as God before then. What happened at the incarnation is that he "took on flesh." Somehow, while remaining fully God, he became fully man as well.[3]

We will explore the implications of the incarnation at the end of this chapter. What you need to see at this moment is that "there was never a time before Christ."[4] History may be divided into B.C. and A.D., but there technically never was a B.C.. Christ had a birth but no beginning. He existed before creation as the Logos – the pre-existent, pre-incarnate Son of God.

His-Story

Given that Jesus has always existed, it follows that he existed throughout the era of the Jewish Scriptures (what Christians refer to as the Old Testament). Most theologians believe he even made a few appearances during this time – e.g., Jesus was one of the three men who spoke with Abraham in Genesis 18, he was the one who accepted the worship of Joshua before the Battle of Jericho in Joshua 5, he was the fourth man in the fire in Daniel 3, etc.

But that is hardly the extent of it. Christians believe that Christ's role in the Old Testament goes far beyond a few cameo appearances - we believe he is the main character. Jesus is the person the prophets talk about, the good kings foreshadow and the temple sacrifices point to. He is the one everyone is looking for whether they realize it or not. Christ may have remained out of reach of the Old Testament stage lights, but he is the still the hero of the story. Everything points to him.

I understand that this may strike some of you as a reckless claim. And I will quickly admit that it can be difficult to see Jesus as the star of the Old Testament at first. There are reasons for this. For starters, the Old Testament is not one book; it's a collection of 39 different ones. In fact, it's a collection of 39 different books that were written in a variety of literary styles over the course of a thousand years by more than two dozen authors. Furthermore, it is not laid out in chronological order. So, it is possible to miss the big picture. More than a few do. But once you realize what you are looking for – once you understand that the Old Testament is not a jump cut of morality tales, religious poetry and words of comfort, but the story of God's plan to redeem mankind – and you actually start looking for a story-line, the pieces come together.[5]

And after they come together, you begin to see Christ on nearly every page. You realize that history really is his-story.

To substantiate this claim, I am going to take you to 30,000 feet and look down on God's unfolding plan. In this chapter we are going to consider the events found in the Old Testament, the 400 years between the end of the Old Testament and the beginning of the New, and also what is contained on the first few pages of the Gospels.

In an effort to make the story as understandable as possible, I am going to return to a metaphor I introduced in FencePosts One – the Bible as a three-act play, complete with Prologue and Intermission.[6]

The Prologue

If we were going to watch the Bible as a play, the information found in Genesis 1 – 11 would be found in the playbill handed to us when we entered the theater. Upon reading it, we would understand the context of what we were going to watch. To be more specific, we would learn that:

- An all-powerful and loving God created mankind in his image, designing them (us) to enjoy a loving relationship with him.[7]

- We rebelled, and as a result were cursed. Everything in our world was ruined by sin.

- The standards of justice are so high, and our debt is so substantial, that we are unable to fix our situation. Unless something changes we are headed towards eternal death, not eternal life.

- Our only hope lies with God. If we are going to be saved, he will need to rescue us.

- He has promised to do just that. He will send "the seed of woman"[8] to defeat evil. There are few details about how this will unfold – certainly not enough to know that the "seed of woman" refers to Jesus. But a promise of some sort has been made, and everything rests upon it.[9]

It is against this backdrop that the lights in the theater dim and the curtain begins to rise.

Act One

The play opens with an offer: God invites a nomadic shepherd named Abraham to a lead role in the most important work of all time. If Abraham is willing to follow God, God will bless him with land and descendents. In fact, God promises to bless the entire world through Abraham.

As was the case in Genesis 3, we are not given enough information at this point to know that this "blessing" refers to the "seed of woman," which in turn refers to Jesus. But that only applies to the first time we read the story! Once we have read the entire Bible through and are able to not only 'read the New Testament in light of the Old,' but also to 'read the Old in light of the New,' we know who they are talking about.

Abraham agrees, and for the next one-thousand pages – i.e., from the offer in Genesis 12 through the rest of the Hebrew Scriptures – we watch as God's plan unfolds. We follow Abraham's descendents (the Jews) as they grow from a family to a tribe, and then from one tribe to twelve. We watch as they leave the land of Promise, enter Egypt, fall into slavery and cry out for freedom (Scene Two). We watch as they regain the land (Scene Three), limp along as a loose confederacy (Scene Four), unite under David (Scene Five) divide after Solomon's death (Scene Six) and are carted into Babylonian exile (Scene Seven). Finally, we are there when a small remnant returns to Jerusalem to start over (Scene 8).

Those who read the Old Testament for the first time are likely to be struck by three things:

- How often the people of God violate the covenant. Abraham's descendents appear unable or unwilling to keep the promises they make to God. They cry out to him for help whenever they are in a bind, but turn away almost as soon as things are going well again.

- How patient and forgiving God is. It's common to suggest that "the God of the Old Testament" is cruel and angry,[10] but those who read the story in context are surprised by the opposite. He comes across as patient, almost to the point of being weak.

- How much blood is spilled. First there are the battles – quite a few of them. But more than that, there are the sacrifices, which never seem to stop.

Once again, I need to stress that one time through is not really enough to understand much of what is going on. But those who finish the Bible and double back again start to notice a number of things they missed the first time.

Messianic Prophecies: For starters, there are a lot of clues about the Messiah. In addition to the Genesis 3 statement describing him as "the seed of woman" – a clear reference to the Virgin Birth – various prophets offer other descriptions (i.e., prophecies) about his life and work. Micah reports that he will be born in Bethlehem. Genesis and Jeremiah specify that he will be from the tribe of Judah and the house of David. The Psalms note that he will be betrayed and describes how he will die. Isaiah notes that though he is poor he will be buried in a rich man's tomb.

The Purpose of the Blood. The longer you read, the more important the blood becomes. Three things in particular come into clearer focus.

- First, the blood of sacrifices operates as a form of currency. In the very beginning God made it clear that sin is a capital offense – that is, when people sin they deserve to die. However, in his mercy God does not require the immediate physical death of guilty parties. He allows innocent third parties (animals) to die so that guilty people can go free. The blood of animals is offered as payment for the moral debt of man.

- Secondly, this trail of blood actually starts to flow before the sacrificial system is ever put in place and it goes on well past it. In fact, it ties together everything from the stories of Cain and Abel, the Binding of Isaac and the Passover with the sacrificial system itself. Some even refer to the flow of the Old Testament as "a crimson thread."

- Finally, the blood of the Old Testament leads all the way to Christ. In the New Testament we learn that the animal blood that was shed on the altar did not actually atone – i.e., pay off – the moral debt of the guilty person, it just served as a place-holder for the future death of Christ which would.

In other words, the entire sacrificial system – which included the deaths of millions of animals over a couple thousand years – was instituted, in effect, to prepare people for the way God would rescue them. God the Father was going to send God the Son as a man in order to die in our place. The death of an innocent man would allow a just God to remain just – evil would be punished – while also allowing a loving God to restore people to himself.

But I am getting ahead of myself. The goal at the moment is to track with the first-time readers, and the biggest take-away they would have after finishing the Old Testament for the first time is that it doesn't end. It just stops. The central question is never resolved. Does God keep his promise or not? Does he send a Messiah or not? Does the "Seed of Woman" arrive to defeat evil or not? The Old Testament ends before we find out.

Of course those who have already read the New Testament know the answer. But the Jews who stumble back from Babylonian captivity do not. They hope so. The prophets encourage them to not give up – they proclaim that God will keep his covenant promises. But things are not looking good. Israel has crashed. She might have enjoyed a meteoric rise to the top and a brief run as a super power, but that was a long, long time ago. The last six hundred years have been downhill – only a remnant of people remain and the temple is a pale shadow of what it had been.

When the curtain falls on Act One God's promises have not been fulfilled and the situation looks bleak.

Binding of Isaac and the Passover with the sacrificial system itself. Some even refer to the flow of the Old Testament as "a crimson thread."

Intermission

There are two very different ways to think about the four hundred years between the end of the Old Testament (Act One) and the beginning of the New (Act Two). On the one hand, we could talk about silence. From a theological perspective, not much happens: prayers are prayed and hope remains – the Jews continued to wait for a Messiah – but the heavens are quiet. God says nothing.

On the other hand, we could look at how many things do change. The political situation is fluid. In the third century B.C., Alexander the Great conquered the known world and brought the Jews under Greek control. Following his death, his generals lost his empire. For a brief period, Israel was ruled by the Syrians, but when they overplayed their hand, Judas Maccabeus led a successful revolt, and for one hundred years the Jews were free. Then Pompey rolled into town, defeated Israel and folded the Jews into Rome's vast empire. [11]

Under Rome, Jewish life grew more difficult.[12] For starters, it meant a stifling amount of governmental control.

- At the very top was the emperor, who not only imposed crippling taxes but who expected to be worshipped as a god.

- Under him was a Roman governor, who commanded the military, authorized construction projects, collected taxes and otherwise looked after Caesar's interests in the region.[13]

- Under the governor was a Jewish king, who was appointed by Caesar to enforce Roman rule at the local level.[14]

- Finally, under these groups was the Sanhedrin, a Jewish council that controlled the people by controlling the courts and the temple. At the time of Christ, two different parties vied for control of the Sanhedrin - the Pharisees and the Sadducees. They seldom cooperated, which made life even more difficult for those they ruled over.[15]

The Jews found the entire situation intolerable.[16] In fact, few groups were as frustrated by Roman rule as they were, and no one gave Rome more trouble. Between 67 B.C. and 37 B.C. no fewer than 150,000 men perished in Palestinian uprisings. The people wanted to be free and were always looking for someone to lead a revolt. As one leading historian has noted, "There was no more explosive and inflammable country in the world than Palestine."[17]

This is the situation into which Christ is born. The typical Jew is struggling under harsh taxes, pagan overlords, oppressive rules and divided leaders. They wanted change. More than that, they believed they were promised as much. Where was their Messiah – the one God had promised to send? Where was the One who would sit on the throne of David forever? Surely he would lead them forward. He would overthrow Rome and lead them back to glory.[18] He was the key to their future.

And many believed he would be arriving soon.[19]

It is at this point that The Intermission ends and the curtain rises for Act II. God is about to break his silence and send the "anointed one." Jesus, who had existed in Heaven as God, is about to enter the world as the God-Man. But his assignment is very different than what the Jews were expecting. He was not coming to overthrow Rome. His kingdom was much grander than that – and not of this world. Consequently, the surprises began with the announcement. It was not made to the political powerbrokers or the religious elite, but to a young peasant girl living in the backwaters of Judea, in the forgotten and despised town of Nazareth.

Act Two Begins

The first to hear about the arrival of the Messiah was Zechariah, an elderly Jewish man living in Judah.[20] In5 B.C. he was performing his duties as a priest when an angel of the Lord appeared to him and announced that his prayers would be answered. [21] Luke 1:11 reads:

> Then an angel of the Lord appeared to him, standing at the right side of the altar of incense. When Zechariah saw him, he was startled and was gripped with fear. But the angel said to him: "Do not be afraid, Zechariah; your prayer has been heard. Your wife Elizabeth will bear

you a son, and you are to call him John. He will be a joy and delight to you, and many will rejoice because of his birth, for he will be great in the sight of the Lord. He is never to take wine or other fermented drink, and he will be filled with the Holy Spirit even before he is born. He will bring back many of the people of Israel to the Lord their God. And he will go on before the Lord, in the spirit and power of Elijah, to turn the hearts of the parents to their children and the disobedient to the wisdom of the righteous—to make ready a people prepared for the Lord."

The next to hear was Mary herself, a young Jewish virgin who was engaged to marry a local carpenter named Joseph.

In the sixth month of Elizabeth's pregnancy, God sent the angel Gabriel to Nazareth, a town in Galilee, to a virgin pledged to be married to a man named Joseph, a descendant of David. The virgin's name was Mary. The angel went to her and said, "Greetings, you who are highly favored! The Lord is with you."

Mary was greatly troubled at his words and wondered what kind of greeting this might be. But the angel said to her, "Do not be afraid, Mary; you have found favor with God. You will conceive and give birth to a son, and you are to call him Jesus. He will be great and will be called the Son of the Most High. The Lord God will give him the throne of his father David, and he will reign over Jacob's descendants forever; his kingdom will never end."

"How will this be," Mary asked the angel, "since I am a virgin?"

"The angel answered, "The Holy Spirit will come on you, and the power of the Most High will overshadow you. So the holy one to be born will be called the Son of God. Even Elizabeth your relative is going to have a child in her old age, and she who was said to be unable to conceive is in her sixth month. For no word from God will ever fail."

"I am the Lord's servant," Mary answered. "May your word to me be fulfilled." Then the angel left her.

There are several things to notice about this passage. For starters, the name God selects for his Son is Jesus – Yeshua in Hebrew – which means "God saves." This was a common name. Indeed, Jesus is frequently referred to as Jesus of Nazareth to distinguish him from all of the other Jesuses of the day.[22] Second, Mary is told that her son will be the most remarkable person to ever live. In fact, she is told that he will be the "Son of God," will occupy the "throne of David," and will establish "a kingdom that does not end." Finally, Mary is told that she will conceive while remaining a virgin.

A Virgin Conception

Given how many people dismiss the Virgin Birth, it's worth noting that the first to express reservations about it was Mary herself.[23] Luke reports that she was frightened by the angel, surprised at being chosen and troubled by how her pregnancy would be viewed by others. Those of us who are accustomed to young women having children out of wedlock are unlikely to appreciate how this news would have played out in a first-century Jewish village. Mary was not. She knew that she could be stoned. She also suspected that her claims to virginity would be dismissed by just about everyone, including her fiancé.[24] For these reasons and perhaps others, Mary sets off to visit her cousin, Elizabeth.

Elizabeth is Zechariah's wife – the very one whose miraculous pregnancy had been announced a few months earlier by the same angel that had just visited Mary. Mary must have realized that if anyone was going to believe her story it would be Elizabeth. And she was right.

It is interesting to imagine the conversations these two women must have had. Mary was probably greatly encouraged by the support and counsel she received from her godly – and much older – Aunt. They had so much in common. But careful readers are struck by the dramatic contrasts.

• Zechariah was excited that Elizabeth was pregnant; Joseph was making plans to divorce Mary.

• The community was celebrating with Elizabeth; but they will soon shun Mary.

The fact that Mary will decide to travel with Joseph to Bethlehem – even though the trip is difficult, she does not need to make it and she is due to deliver at any moment – suggests just how bad things would get for her in Nazareth.[25]

The Birth of Christ

Given the cosmic significance of what happens next, the reports we find in the Gospels are almost comical. Matthew spends most of his first chapter chronicling Christ's genealogy. He is then so busy emphasizing that Joseph did not sleep with Mary until after Christ was born, that the announcement of God's birth is not even the main subject of the sentence.[26]

Luke's account is similar. He starts by explaining how Caesar's census forced Joseph to return to Bethlehem, notes that Mary goes with him, and then states, "while they were there, the time came for the baby to be born, and she gave birth to her firstborn, a son."

Mark and John skip the story altogether.[27]

Perhaps this is one case where less is more. Or perhaps this is one spot where words simply fail.

What can be said? In the most remarkable act of humility possible, the creator of ten billion galaxies became a small and helpless infant. He did so through the womb of a teenage mother. He arrived in a barn behind a small inn.[28] With the exception of a host of angels and a few shepherds, the event went unnoticed.[29]

Again, perhaps this is one case where words simply fail. Or perhaps all that needs to be said is that God became man. He did not put on a costume and act like a person – he really became a human baby.[30] He stooped that low.

Jesus is The One

Unlike modern biographies, the Gospels provide few details about Christ's childhood. Between the four different accounts, only three events are mentioned.[31] But these three are quite important. Two are clearly recounted in order to persuade the reader that Jesus is The One.

- **First, the infant is recognized by Simeon and Anna:** Eight days
  after Jesus was born he was circumcised, named[32] and taken to the
  Temple to be dedicated to God.[33] While there, Mary and Joseph were
  approached by two strangers. The first was Simeon, an old man who
  believed that he would not die until he beheld the Messiah. After
  taking Jesus in his arms, Simeon told the Lord that he was ready "to
  be dismissed in peace, for my eyes have seen your salvation."[34]

  The other who paid special attention to the newborn was an older
  woman named Anna. Luke reports that when she saw Jesus she "gave
  thanks to God and spoke about the child to all who were looking
  forward to the redemption of Jerusalem."[35]

- **Second, Jesus is worshipped by the Magi:** Between a bright star and
  some Old Testament prophecies, a caravan of Persian astronomers
  was able to find its way to Bethlehem to visit the baby.[36] By stopping
  at Herod's palace to ask for directions the Magi inadvertently alerted
  Herod to a new rival. But what is most important about this text is
  that it shows that wise men from another land recognized Jesus as the
  fulfillment of prophecy and worshipped him as God. [37]

When the wise men failed to report back to the palace with the location of
the new king, Herod dispatched troops to Bethlehem to kill every Jewish
boy under the age of two.[38] But the soldiers were too late to murder Jesus.
Having been warned in a dream that his adopted son was in danger, Joseph
had already taken Mary and Jesus and fled to Egypt. They remained there
until Herod's death.[39]

Jesus as a Young Boy

The Gospels provide even fewer details about Christ's childhood than they
do about his birth.[40] We know that after returning from Egypt, Mary, Joseph
and Jesus settled in Nazareth[41] where Joseph worked as a builder. We also
know that Jesus ended up with at least four brothers and one sister.

Beyond that, we can assume that their life was simple. After all, there were only a few hundred people living in Nazareth at that time, and Joseph's job provided a lower- to middle-class standard of living – i.e., they probably lived in a mud-brick home with dirt floors.[42]

We can also assume that Jesus received a basic education. Most Jewish boys learned to read and write from their mother and learned a trade from their father. There is no reason to think that Jesus was different. It's also probable that he attended classes in the local synagogue. (It is here where he worked to memorize the Torah[43] and learn to correctly interpret the Law and Prophets.)

The only glimpse we are given of his life between his birth and his emergence as a rabbi thirty years later occurs when he was twelve. The residents of Bethlehem had celebrated the Passover in Jerusalem and were returning home when Mary and Joseph realized that Jesus was not among the travel party. They retraced their steps and eventually found him at the Temple, where he was amazing the religious leaders with his wisdom and knowledge.

Based on this event it seems safe to say that, in many ways, Jesus was a normal boy. The fact that his parents did not start looking for him until he had been out of their sight for at least a day suggests that he spent most of his time with friends.

But in other ways Jesus was already quite exceptional. While there is no suggestion that he hovered six inches off the ground or wore a halo, most twelve year old boys are not noted for their religious insights. Nor do they refer to God with the intimacy Christ displayed. When Mary expressed her frustration over the grief Jesus had caused them by going missing, he asked her:

> "Why were you searching for me? Didn't you know I had to be in my Father's house?"

Those familiar with the opening of the Lord's Prayer – "Our Father, who art in Heaven" – miss the force of this statement. Before Christ's response to Mary no one had ever referred to God as "My Father." The holy, righteous, almighty creator of Heaven and Earth was occasionally referred to as "The

Father of the Nation of Israel," but not as "My Father." Jesus is the first to ever refer to him in this way.[44]

The Silent Years

The eighteen years between the Passover event just described and Christ's baptism hardly compare to the 400 years between the end of the Old Testament and the beginning of the New, but they are just as silent. The Bible does not tell us anything about what went on in Christ's life during this time.

Can we speculate? Sure. It seems safe to assume that it was during these years that Joseph died, and that as the oldest son, Jesus worked to help Mary raise her other children.[45] Additionally, given the stories Jesus will tell later on, it's likely that he spent these years in a small village.

We can also wonder. Did Christ's responsibilities at home keep him from the advanced training available to the brightest students? Did he hear stories about his Mom's claim to be a virgin when he was born? How much of his mission did he understand at this time?[46] We can ask lots of questions, but we cannot answer many of them, for both the Bible and history are silent.

It appears as though Jesus was waiting for something to happen. And that "something" was the emergence of his cousin from the desert. The next move was not his to make. It rested with John the Baptist.

We will pick up there in the next study, which will focus on the three years between Christ's baptism and his final march into Jerusalem. But before we do, I want to go back to 30,000 feet and make sure the remarkable claims we've covered so far are understood in context. I realize that you may not believe them, but it's critical that we at least understand the story that is being told.

The View from 30,000 Feet

The Incarnation: The central claim of the Christian faith is that the child conceived in Mary's womb was God the Son, and that he became a man in order to rescue you and me. This claim is comprised of a handful of tenets, including the following:

- Shortly after the Fall, God the Father promised that he would send His Son – the seed of woman – to defeat evil, redeem man and restore His kingdom.

- The Old Testament is the story of God's plan to honor this promise. After a brief introduction (The Prologue), we learn that the Savior will be a descendent of Abraham. We then watch as Abraham's offspring grows from a single family into a powerful nation, and then slides backwards into obscurity and near oblivion. During their rise and fall the Jews not only learn a great deal about God's character, they are also given a number of veiled descriptions – i.e., prophecies – about the future Messiah.

- Most of the Jews believe that the Messiah they are waiting for will look and act much like King David – i.e., he will defeat Rome and restore Jewish political prominence. They long for his arrival.

- The New Testament opens with two angelic announcements. Zechariah is told that his wife will give birth to the one who will "prepare the way for the Messiah." Mary is told that she will give birth to the Messiah himself. Mary later gives birth to Jesus.

- Jesus is the One the Jews were waiting for. He is God himself and always has been. He existed with the Father and Spirit before the creation of the world.

- At the moment of the incarnation, Jesus humbled himself in order to become a man. Somehow, while remaining fully God he became fully man. From that point forward he is one person with two natures. He took these extraordinary steps in order to redeem us.

- The Gospel writers tell us little about Jesus' early years, but the few glimpses we are given reinforce the idea that he is the Messiah.

Vere Deus Vere Homus: How did this happen? How could the finite and infinite co-mingle in one man? How could Jesus be God and still be a real person? The answer is: we do not know. The incarnation stands alongside the Trinity as one of the great mysteries of the Christian faith. We can think about it all we'd like, but a full understanding of God's nature lies beyond us. Finitum non capex infiniti – the finite cannot fully comprehend the infinite.

This does not mean that we are unable to say anything. In fact, the early church said a fair bit. Shortly after the bishops gathered to defend Christ's deity – a series of meetings that gave us the Nicene Creed – they gathered for a second set of meetings to defend his humanity. This second set of meetings resulted in the Chalcedonian Definition, a document that makes it clear that since the incarnation Jesus has been (and will always remain) fully God and fully man.[47] He was not half god and half man, a god who merely looked like a man, a man who merely acted like god, a god who stopped being God when he became man, or a being who was God part of the time and man the rest.[48]

As you can tell, there are lots of different ways people had misstated Christ's nature. In Chalcedon they made four points very clear:

- Jesus has always been fully God.

- At the time of the incarnation he added humanity to deity.

- He did the second without compromising the first. That is, he added manhood to Godhood without diminishing Godhood in any way. And he did the first without compromising the second. That is, though he remained fully God he became fully man.

- Since that time he has always been both fully man and fully God (vere Deus vere Homus) – one person with two natures.[49]

At the incarnation Jesus becomes one person with two natures: one human and one divine. It's a profound miracle, greater in many ways than the resurrection.

This Changes Everything

Discussions about something as profound as the incarnation can leave us feeling a bit overwhelmed. That's understandable. You will not ponder anything this week as vexing as the dual nature of the Son of God. But, feeling overwhelmed should not be your only response. If the Bible gives us an accurate account of reality – and I believe it does – then God's plan to reveal himself as a human is among the best news you are ever going to hear. It changes everything.

For starters it means we can know what God is like. We can go beyond saying what he is not – i.e., He is not mortal; He is not finite; He is not visible, etc. The incarnation allows us to say what He is: the Father is like the Son. His love for you is like the love of a man who lays down his life for a friend.

Secondly, it means that God wants to be known. He was so determined to be known by you that he set aside some of the honor he was due in order to take on human form. This cosmic downsizing is almost as incomprehensible as Christ's nature! Do not listen to those who suggest that God becoming man is like man becoming an ant – it's 10,000,000 times greater than that. God made us out of nothing. We cannot make an ant. We cannot even start with the parts and put them together. The Creator became part of creation in order to be known by you.

Thirdly, it means he understands. He doesn't pretend to know the challenges you face, he faced them. Jesus did not stay behind the battle lines; he went into the worst situations. He faced every heartbreak and every temptation you ever will. The incarnation means that Christ does not empathize with our situation, he sympathizes with it.

Finally, it means Christ can represent us in death. A full explanation of this point will have to wait, but it deserves to be introduced here. There are several reasons why Jesus became a man, but the central one is this: we needed someone who could take our place in death. As a man, Jesus is qualified to represent us – he can act as our substitute. As God, his death is of infinite value – he is able to die for you, me and everyone else who follows him. The incarnation makes our salvation possible.

ENDNOTES

[1] The Christian claim is that one God exists in three persons and that Jesus is the second person in this tri-unity, God the Son. For a more complete exploration of the doctrine of the Trinity please see FencePosts 2.2.

[2] John actually goes beyond claiming that the Logos pre-existed the cosmos. His claim is that the Logos created the cosmos. Edgar Lovelady, author of The Logos Concept, paraphrases John 1:1 this way: "At the initiation of time, when the creation of the world took place, the Logos (the pre-existent, pre-incarnate Son of God, who personally intervened in the cosmos for the purposes of creation, preservation, and revelation) this Logos was already with God the Father, and this same Word was the essence of God in the most absolute sense." The Logos Concept: A Critical Monograph, (Grace Theological Journal, Spring, 1963), p. 15-24.

[3] The term incarnation is derived from the Latin word carnos, which means "flesh" or "meat." (Chili con carne is chili with meat in it.) It means that Jesus became God with "meat on his bones."

[4] The line "there was never a time before Christ" was first made by the Early Church Fathers. Also, at the risk of confusing you, I need to note that the Bible does not claim that Jesus has always existed, but rather that the Son of God – the Second Person of the Trinity – has always existed. Jesus is the human name given to the second person of the Trinity after he took on flesh. He was not called "Jesus" until Joseph called him that after his birth.

[5] A story is told about a children's sermon in which the pastor asks if anyone knows what is small, fury, climbs trees and has a bushy tail. One young boy responds, "I know the answer is Jesus but it sure sounds like a squirrel." I want to be clear, the first thing we seek to do when reading the Old Testament is to seek to understand what the writer wanted the original reader to understand. We do not simply say "Jesus" and move on. It is only after we have read / analyzed a given passage in its initial, historical setting that we should prayerfully place it in its biblical-theological context in the flow of redemptive history.

[6] A more robust explanation of the Bible as a three-act play can be found in FencePosts 1.4 and 1.5.

⁷ I am using personal pronouns here because the claim is that the story is actually our story.

⁸ This term appears to refer to one who is conceived without a male seed. It is discussed at greater length in the final chapter.

⁹ The Prologue sets up the central question: will God rescue mankind, and if so, when and how? It unfolds as follows: 1) Genesis 1 & 2 describes a world that is wonderful; 2) Genesis 3 reports on the Fall, the destruction that it brings, the curse and God's promise to send help; 3) Genesis 4 - 6 showcases just how bad mankind has become (Cain kills Abel, human wickedness increases, etc); 4) In Genesis 6 &7 evil is so rampant that God mercifully floods the world and essentially starts again with one family; 5) Genesis 9 shows that the darkness in man's heart is once again going to infect everything that follows. If you read the Prologue thoughtfully you are left with a sense of despair. Mankind is not going to be able to make things right. The only hope rests with God. Will he keep his promise?

¹⁰ Some even go so far as to pit "the angry God of the Old Testament" against the loving example of Jesus. The first to do so was a second-century heretic named Marcion, thus this heresy is called Marcionism.

¹¹ In an effort to force the Jews to embrace Greek culture, General Antiochus Epiphanies desecrated the temple by slaughtering a pig in the Holy of Holies. But rather than acquiesce, the Jews revolted and regained their independence. (Hanukkah is a celebration of this victory). Their freedom lasted until 63 B.C., when Pompey conquered the land and folded Palestine into the Roman Empire. At the time of Christ, Roman rule extended as far west as what is now known as Spain, as far south as the northern tip of Africa, as far north as Asia Minor and modern Germany, and as far east as Judea. Scholars estimate that around 1 A.D. the total population of the Roman Empire was between 50 and 60 million people.

¹² First century Palestinian life may not have been as difficult as you envision, even under Roman rule. People still fell in love, got married and raised families. Kids still climbed trees, went to school and learned how to read and write. Most people lived in towns or cities, paid taxes and obeyed the law. Larger metropolitan areas had hotels, libraries, theaters and restaurants, not to mention roads, sewage systems and police officers. Ancient life may not have been as ancient as you are thinking. Of course it was less developed than today. Little of the technology we take for granted was available – by which I do not mean jet travel, GPS units and smart phones, but light bulbs, refrigerators and washing machines. Newspapers were unheard of, books were handwritten and medicine was in its infancy. In fact, a first century doctor did more harm than good. Fevers, infections

and allergic reactions were often fatal, and many women (and children) died during childbirth. Historians estimate the average life expectancy in Ancient Rome at 25. (Nara Schoenberg, The Buck Stops Here, Chicago Tribune, Saturday, June 4, 2011, p. 16).

[13] During most of Christ's life the Roman governor – who was also called a prefect – was Pontius Pilate.

[14] At the time of Christ's birth, Herod the Great – the first in a line of Herods – was king. He had been appointed in 40 B.C. by Mark Anthony and would stay in that spot until his death in 4 B.C. Though not a Jew by birth, Herod converted to Judaism, married into a prominent Jewish family and rebuilt the Temple. Nevertheless, among those he ruled he was never ultimately accepted as being one of them. The insecurities that resulted likely contributed to his pathological behavior. He not only ordered the "Slaughter of the Innocents," but had his wife, two sons and an uncle murdered when he suspected them of aspiring to his position. (Caesar Augustus subsequently reported that it would be better to be Herod's pig than his son.) Remarkably, he was as gifted as he was cruel. His building campaigns were so extraordinary that some historians believe he would have had title to half of the Seven Wonders of the World if he'd been born one hundred years earlier.

[15] By the time of Christ's ministry, the Jews had actually splintered into four parties, dividing largely over their responses to Roman occupation. The Zealots defied Rome. They saw themselves as "freedom fighters." (Simon, one of Christ's disciples, was a Zealot.) The Sadducees cooperated with Rome. A religiously liberal, largely aristocratic minority, they held power over the Sanhedrin by currying favor with Herod. The Essenes sought to avoid all contact with Rome by retreating into the desert to await the apocalypse. (The Essenes gained notoriety in the 1940s after the Dead Sea Scrolls were found in one of their ancient communities.) The final group was the Pharisees, religious hardliners whose political views were shaped by their desire to regulate the life of the Jewish people. Those who joined this party believed that every situation should be scripted by either the Hebrew Bible or their ever-expanding canon of rules. They are the most well known to today's readers because of their frequent clashes with Jesus.

[16] On top of this was Rome's view of the value of life – to them it was cheap. One-third of the people living in their empire were slaves, public executions were swift and numerous, and instead of watching football on weekends they liked to watch gladiators kill each other or prisoners get fed to wild animals.

[17] As noted, there were many uprisings. In 4 B.C. the city of Sepphoris,

just a short walk from Nazareth, was the site of a revolt and was burned to the ground. Rome crucified 2,000 of the Jewish men who participated in that uprising. Things were not finally resolved until after the Jewish revolt launched in 70 A.D. was put down and Jerusalem was destroyed. (It took Rome three years to prevail in that situation, and they were so frustrated with the Jews by the time it was over that they not only destroyed the Jewish temple and massacred thousands, they demolished Jerusalem itself, drove the Jews away and renamed the land.) (The reference is from William Barclay. It is cited in The Jesus I Never Knew, p. 57.)

[18] When an earthquake in Palestine killed 30,000 Jews in 31 B.C., most viewed it as "pangs of the Messiah" and pleaded for his arrival.

[19] Biblical prophecies are easier to understand after the fact than before. They are written in such a way that they are very clear once they have been fulfilled, but prior to that you are left wondering. As a result, there were several different understandings of the type of person the Messiah would be. A few expected a great priest, a few others thought he would be a prophet, and there were even some who thought that he would be a supernatural being. The prevailing view, however – and certainly the view embraced by the man on the street – was that the Messiah would be like David, a warrior king who would exercise political and military leadership. (Jesus uniquely fulfills all of the expectations.)

[20] The exact date of Christ's birth is impossible to establish given the information we currently have, and the arguments being debated are too technical to take up here. But two things are worth noting: 1) We have little reason to think the birth takes place on December 25th – which is the date selected by Constantine in the fourth century – because the shepherds would have been unlikely to be out in their fields at night in the winter; 2) Besides the day and month being difficult to establish, the exact year is a bit of a challenge as well. Records indicate that Herod the Great died in 4 B.C. Based on this well-established date, most scholars believe that Jesus was born in 5 B.C. or 6 B.C.

[21] We are not certain what Zechariah had been praying for. It may have been for a son. It may have been for God to send "Elijah" to announce that the Messiah would soon follow, or it may have been for the Messiah to arrive.

[22] Because the Romans controlled Palestine, and because the Romans had embraced Greek culture, Jesus and his family would have used the Greek language a good part of the time. In Greek, the Hebrew name Yeshua would have been translated Iesous. The name Jesus is a modern, Anglicized version of the Greek name. Yeshua himself would never have heard his

name pronounced GEE-zuhs, as we do today.

23 I comment at length on the Virgin Birth in the Q & A section in the final study. At this point let me simply note: 1) It is nearly impossible to make sense of the rest of the story if you dismiss the virgin conception, for Jesus does not claim to be a good man, he claims to be God; and 2) It should not surprise us that the Son of God enters the world in a unique way. For starters, he already exists. Secondly, he must become human without becoming infected with the sin that mars the rest of the human race.

24 Both Mary's "song" (i.e., The Magnificat, which is found in Luke 1:46-55) and her subsequent life suggest that Mary is a wonderful model of faith.

25 I recently made this trip in the back of a taxi. And at an average speed of close to 70 mph it took us two and a half hours. (When I asked how long it would take on a donkey, I was told that a few years ago a couple set out to recreate the journey. While they were traveling, the donkey died.)

26 Matt. 1:24f reads, "When Joseph woke up, he did what the angel of the Lord had commanded him to do and took Mary home as his wife. But he did not consummate their marriage until she gave birth to a son. And he gave him the name Jesus."

27 Mark begins with John the Baptist's ministry. John opens with a description of Christ that is both cosmic and majestic, but he has nothing to say about the birth itself.

28 Several theories have been advanced to explain why no one had mercy on a young woman in labor: 1) Bethlehem was completely overrun with visitors there for the census. Truly, every room was taken. This was the best that could be offered; 2) Judean Jews were not willing to help someone from Galilee – a "socially inferior" area; and 3) the scandal surrounding Mary's pregnancy preceded her arrival. Of these, the first seems the most plausible. However, in recent years another idea has been suggested. In Jesus Through Middle Eastern Eyes: Cultural Studies in the Gospels, Dr. Kenneth Bailey suggests that the first century homes in Bethlehem included a manger at one end and that the animals were brought into the home at night. If this is true then it would suggest that, though bleak, things were not quite as desperate as believed. However, even if Christ's birth took place inside the walls of a simple home, we cannot help but note the irony: Far from being welcomed as King of Kings, the Lord God Almighty spent his first night next to donkeys and sheep. This is but the first in a long list of ways he was mistreated and humiliated.

29 Shepherds were so low on the social spectrum that their testimony was

not admissible in a court of law.

30 When John says that "the Word became flesh and dwelt among us" (John 1:14), the term he uses for flesh is sarx, an earthy term that refers to human nature in its totality: body, soul, spirit, will, emotions, etc. The Bible speaks of Jesus "coming in the flesh" (I Jn 4:2; 2 Jn 7), being "sent in the flesh" (Rom. 8:3), "appearing in the flesh" (I Tim 3:16), "suffering in the flesh" (I Peter 4:1), etc. In sum, the Word became flesh.

31 It is worth noting that two of these three events were designed to show that Jesus was the promised Messiah.

32 There are a few points worth noting about names in general and Christ's names in particular: 1) Jesus has one name and many titles – e.g., Jesus is his name, Christ is a title. Many mistakenly think Christ is Jesus' last name, but Christos is the Greek translation of the Hebrew term, Messiah, which means, "anointed one." Initially Jesus was called "Jesus the Christ," but over time the definite article was dropped; 2) All of his titles are significant because God reveals various truths through them. Jesus means "God saves," Emmanuel means "God is with us"; 3) God the Father, not Mary or Joseph, chose Christ's name, because naming someone is an act of power over them, and neither Mary nor Joseph had that power over Jesus.

33 As the first born male in a Jewish family, Jesus was ceremonially "given" to God (Ex. 13:1-2, 12). The service would not be unlike an infant baptism or dedication service today.

34 Simeon's full prayer was, "Sovereign Lord, as you have promised, you may now dismiss your servant in peace. For my eyes have seen your salvation, which you have prepared in the sight of all nations: a light for revelation to the Gentiles, and the glory of your people Israel." (Luke 2:29ff). After praying Simeon blessed Mary and Joseph and then said the following to her: "This child is destined to cause the falling and rising of many in Israel, and to be a sign that will be spoken against, so that the thoughts of many hearts will be revealed. And a sword will pierce your own soul too." The last line would certainly have had a chilling effect on Mary. But upon Christ's crucifixion, Simeon's words proved true.

35 Luke 2:36ff

36 Based on numerous children's skits, many conclude that there were three magi, and that they showed up ten minutes after Christ was born wearing terrycloth bathrobes. It is likely that a much larger contingent showed up, and that it was at least a month after Christ's birth before they arrived.

[37] We may honor others, but the Bible is quite clear that we should only worship God.

[38] This is referred to as the Slaughter of the Innocents.

[39] It's possible that Joseph obtained work in Egypt and supported the family there for some time. It's also possible that they were away for only a brief period and were able to fund their stay from the gifts Jesus had received from the Magi.

[40] Some, such as the Gnostics, have filled these years with fictional accounts of Jesus as a young boy. In The Infancy Gospel of Thomas we read a few stories about Jesus performing whimsical and frivolous miracles as a young child. But there is no reason to think they are true. Given how late these Gnostic gospels were written – and the curious agenda they promote – few besides tabloid editors treat them seriously.

[41] Nazareth has several things working against it: 1) It was a little country town in the hills, barely larger than a village; 2) it was in the region of Galilee, which good Jews thought of as half pagan; 3) it has no claim to fame or great historical associations. Thus, when Philip told his brother that he wanted him to meet this most amazing man "from Nazareth," Nathaniel responded, "Can any good thing come from Nazareth?" (John 1:45-49)

[42] I am not suggesting that Christ had a middle-class standard of living throughout his life. When Mary and Joseph dedicated him at the temple, the sacrifice they offered indicated that they were poor. Also, after he began his work as a rabbi, he and the disciples lived very modestly.

[43] The Torah refers to the first five books of the Bible – Genesis, Exodus, Leviticus, Numbers and Deuteronomy. These are also referred to as the Pentateuch. They were all written principally by Moses.

[44] God was understood to be the Father of the Nation of Israel, but not Father of a person per se, and certainly not Abba (Dad), which Christ will use later on. This is our first hint from Christ himself that he is more than a normal boy.

[45] We do not hear about Joseph after Christ's visit to the Temple around his twelfth birthday. Beyond that, in Mark 6:3 Jesus is referred to as 'the son of Mary' by residents of Nazareth. Given that they do not recognize his claims to be God, there is no reason to think they are recognizing Mary's claim to a virgin conception. It would be odd in that day for them to refer to Jesus as Mary's son even if Joseph were dead. It seems unthinkable that they would do so if he were alive.

[46] It seems certain that Jesus would have been aware of the stories surrounding his mother – i.e., the visits by an angel, the claim of a virgin conception, etc. But we are not told how much he understood about his mission during his youth.

[47] During the three hundred years following Christ's death it was illegal to be a Christian. This made it impossible for church leaders to meet together and formalize any aspects of their faith. When Constantine became Emperor he rescinded this law and invited all of the bishops to meet together in Nicea. One of the most pressing issues facing the bishops at that time was the teaching of Arius, a charismatic leader who claimed that Jesus was not fully God. The bishops responded by issuing the Nicene Creed which was written to affirm that Christ is fully divine. The Definition of Chalcedon, which was written in 451 A.D. and which is also called the Chalcedonian Creed, came in response to confusion over Christ's humanity. When the bishops met to resolve this issue everyone agreed that Jesus needed to be God in order to save and that he needed to be man in order to represent mankind, but they disagreed on the mechanics and specifics of "one person with two natures." Some emphasized his humanity, arguing that man must know that God has entered history and can fully understand us and relate to our struggles. Others emphasized his deity, arguing that we must know that in Christ we meet the all-powerful God of the universe. The arguments they made were technical and not that important at the moment. What is important is that they were able to resolve their differences by emphasizing the essentials – i.e., Jesus Christ is fully divine and fully human – without trying to describe exactly how that relationship works. The definition they agreed upon employs a technical term that was common at the time. In English this term is translated hypostatic and it means "of one substance." Thus, the Chalcedonian Creed affirms that Jesus is 'of one substance' with God, just as he is 'of one substance' with man.

[48] There are at least a half dozen different views that the Chalcedonian Definition was written to rebuff: 1) The Docetists, who said Jesus was God but not man; 2) the Adoptionists, who said that Jesus was a man who was adopted by God at the time of his baptism; 3) the Modalists, who argued that Jesus and God are one person – i.e., they deny the Trinity; 4) the Arians, who argued that Jesus was a man and god-like, but not fully god; 5) the Apollinarians, who held that Jesus was one person with one nature (not two); and 6) the Nestorians, who claimed that Jesus was fully God and fully man but not one person.

[49] The Chalcedonian Definition states that Jesus "is perfect in Godhead and also perfect in manhood; truly God and truly man." It goes on to add that his two natures are: "without confusion, without change, without division and without separation."

50

[50] Oxford Theologian Alister McGrath notes that Jesus is like a window that allows some of God's light to shine into our world. The window may not be as large or as clean (I Cor. 13:12) as we would like, but God is made available to us. He goes on to write, "The image of Christ facing the cross on our behalf connects with us in ways 'An infinite God of infinite love' does not. It shows us that his love is not a soft, sentimental propositional truth. It is real. It is costly. It doesn't blink. It overcomes. The highest, grandest most complete revelation of God the Father is God the Son. Jesus is 'the radiance of God's glory and the exact representation of his being.'" (Heb. 1:3). See Alister McGrath, Understanding Jesus, chapters 6 & 7.

[51] In a later chapter we will address the charge that Christ is not God, nor does he claim to be. But let's not miss the irony present here. Some ask, "Is Christ divine?" as if they have an understanding of what divine looks like, while suggesting that Christ is something of an enigma. The exact opposite is the case. Christ is tangible and visible. In the Gospels we listen to him speak and watch how he interacts with people. He is on display. In contrast, we have no clear idea about God. As John's Gospel reminds us, "No one has ever seen God, but the one and only Son, who is himself God and is in closest relationship with the Father, has made him known." (John 1:18). Jesus shows us what God is like.

[52] We cannot make an ant. We can't even start with the parts of an ant and put one together. Humans and ants are both creatures. God is the creator. The difference between types of creatures – i.e., humans and ants – is small compared to the gulf between God and mankind. Christ gave up the glory of heaven in order to become a helpless infant and eventually suffer and die.

[53] The literal meaning of the word sympathetic is to "suffer along side." It's from the Greek syn- (together) and pathos (feelings).

CHAPTER 3
Jesus the Christ- From Baptism to Triumphal Entry

A historian like myself, who doesn't even call himself a Christian, finds the picture centering irresistibly around the life and character of this most significant man... The historian's test of an individual's greatness is, 'What did he leave to grow?' Did he start men thinking along fresh lines with a vigor that persisted after him? By this test Jesus stands first.

H.G. Wells

For in Christ all the fullness of the Deity lives in bodily form.

The Apostle Paul

It's worth stating that if you are neutral or ambivalent about Christ, you have not understood his claims or demands. There are many gentle souls out there – "generous philanthropists, high-minded reformers and altruistic social workers. Long may they continue." Jesus was not one of them. He did not claim to be one of them and he did not act like one of them. Had he, we could look on with some interest, be encouraged and walk away. Christ made demands.

R. T. France

Fundamentally, our Lord's message was Himself. He did not come merely to preach a Gospel; He himself is that Gospel. He did not come merely to give bread; He said, "I am the bread". He did not come merely to shed light; He said, "I am the light". He did not come merely to point the way; He said, "I am the way, the truth, and the life".

J. Sidlow Baxter

Two things quickly become obvious to anyone attempting to summarize Christ's life. The first is, it's already been done. Mark's Gospel is only 22 pages long. Matthew, Luke and John's are each a bit longer, but not much. When you realize that Richard Nixon's autobiography approaches 1,200 pages, and that William Manchester's treatise on Churchill approaches three thousand, you realize that 22 pages is not many. When it comes to the Gospels, we are already dealing with the Cliffs Notes.

The second thing is, further cuts will be difficult. Painfully so. If you think I'm wrong, grab a red pen and see how many lines you can cross out. My guess is, you'll reach the same conclusion I did. Each story is fresh. Every parable is powerful. It all needs to stay.

I am convinced that the writers of the Apostle's Creed knew exactly what they were doing when they jumped from "born of the Virgin Mary" to "suffered under Pontius Pilate" without saying anything about what happened in between. They were among the first to realize, once you say anything about Jesus, it's hard not to say a lot more.

But it's a summary we are after. In part because you are unlikely to read 1,200 pages, but chiefly because a well-crafted overview can help us see things we might otherwise miss. What follows is an effort to summarize Christ's adult life. It's longer than the Apostle's Creed, but mercifully shorter than Manchester's work. We'll focus on the three years of Christ's public ministry, starting with John the Baptist's advance work and ending with his entry into Jerusalem just days before he was killed.

John the Baptist

The first thing you need to know about "John the Baptizer" is that everyone was waiting for him. In the last words of the last paragraph of the last book of the Old Testament – Malachi 4 – the Jews were given a description of the events that would unfold immediately prior to the Messiah's arrival. Malachi reported that, just before "the great and awesome Day of the Lord," God would send Elijah to "turn the hearts of fathers to their children and the hearts of children to their fathers."

The Jews had been waiting a long time for this prophecy to be fulfilled. In 28 AD – four hundred years after Malachi told them to start looking – a man walked out of the desert, stepped onto the banks of the Jordan River and began to preach. "Elijah" had finally arrived.[1] His name was John the Baptist.

As prophets go, John was right out of central casting[2] – he wore camel skin clothes, ate large bugs and spoke with thundering conviction. His message was as arresting as his appearance. He told the Jews that God was about to do something remarkable, but that they would be left behind unless they changed the way they were living. It was no longer enough to be Abraham's physical descendants. God could raise those up from the rocks if he wanted to.[3] The people of God needed to repent and be baptized.

This was unexpected. In fact, it was offensive. Sure, Gentile converts needed special cleansing, but not God's own people. Besides, the Law already had guidelines for dealing with sin and they centered around the Temple. For "the Baptizer" to suggest that everyone needed to wade into the Jordan was both confusing and insulting.[4]

But that was John's message. And in spite of its harshness, people responded. As word spread that a prophet had emerged from the desert and was calling Jews to repent, thousands turned out to hear what he had to say. Maybe the Messiah had finally arrived! Perhaps, after all these years, something was actually about to happen.

Among those paying close attention to the prophet's message was a delegation from the Sanhedrin. One of their number eventually put the question to John directly: "Are you the Messiah?"

"I am not," he reported. But what he said next did little to dampen anyone's hopes. He announced that he had been sent by God to prepare for The One they had been waiting for – one so important, powerful and holy that John was not fit to touch this person's shoelaces.

The Messiah was about to appear.

The Baptism and Testing of Jesus

It's at this point that Jesus, John's cousin, walks onto center stage – a spot he will occupy for the rest of the Gospels. Two steps remain before he can begin his mission. First, he must be baptized. To that end he walks into the Jordan River and approaches John. When the prophet spotted Jesus he immediately proclaimed, "Behold the Lamb of God who takes away the sins of the world," and began pleading with Christ to switch places with him. John argued that Jesus should baptize him, not the other way around. But Christ refused. He explained that it was necessary for him to be baptized "in order to fulfill all righteousness." John eventually acquiesced and lowered Jesus into the Jordan.

As Christ emerged from the water the heavens parted, the Spirit descended upon Him as a dove and His Father's voice cried out, "This is my Son, whom I love; with him I am well pleased." Theologians underline these verses because they are so profoundly Trinitarian – that is, they show the Father, Son and Holy Spirit in one place. But we should underline them for a different reason: this is Christ's commissioning. His work is about to begin.

The second act of preparation was a test. After stepping out of the river, Christ was led into the desert by the Holy Spirit. He remained there for forty days, fasting and praying. Towards the end of that time – when he was weak with hunger – Satan tried to divert him from his mission by offering Him, "all the kingdoms of this world."[5]   More significantly, he offered Christ a future that did not include the cross. But Jesus refused. No one had successfully survived this kind of frontal attack before. Not Adam. Not Abraham and certainly not Israel. But Jesus did.[6] He had been sent for a reason. He would not be diverted. He maintained his righteousness even in the midst of this focused attack.

Luke ends this section by noting, "When the devil had ended every temptation, he departed from him 'until an opportune time.'"[7] Jesus would face more challenges, but this one was behind him. Christ was ready to start preaching. His days as a carpenter were over. It was time to announce that the Kingdom of God was at hand.

Rabbi Jesus

Before we begin following Christ on his preaching tour, it's necessary to say a few things about his role as a teacher. Because the Hebrew Scriptures were so important to the Jewish people – and because they needed to be able to read them in order to understand and apply them – first century Jews were among the most educated people of their day. Jewish children were taught to read and write at an early age, and young boys were enrolled in classes to study "the Law and the Prophets." Additionally, every male was expected to memorize the Torah – i.e., Genesis, Exodus, Leviticus, Numbers and Deuteronomy – before they turned twelve. In fact, only those who had memorized the entire Old Testament before they turned fourteen were allowed to train to become a rabbi.[8]

From what we can tell, Christ's formal academic training was limited. It appears as though Joseph died when Jesus was in his teens and that as the oldest son Jesus needed to work to help Mary support and raise her other children. Therefore, he did not have the opportunity to study full time. While others were apprenticing under a rabbi, Jesus was working as a carpenter. Nevertheless, he not only became a rabbi around his thirtieth birthday, he quickly emerged as one of the most popular teachers in Galilee. It wasn't long before everyone in Israel was talking about the remarkable young teacher from Nazareth.

What made Jesus unique? Why did he create such a buzz? Why did so many people turn out to hear what he had to say? Those of us who started reading at the beginning of Act One – and who realize that Jesus is the Logos, the eternal Son of God – already know. We are not surprised that Jesus "wows the crowds." After all, he's not just a man among boys, he is God among men. But his first century listeners did not know this, and it would be a while before anyone figured it out. The crowds that initially gathered to hear Jesus speak were not there because they thought he was God, they were fascinated by him for three other reasons.

First: The Quality of His Life. Jesus was different. Rabbis generally climbed up the social ladder. Jesus moved in the opposite direction. He cared for those others overlooked. In fact, he cared for those others despised. He not only treated women as equals, Jesus partied with tax collectors, honored Samaritans, defended prostitutes and touched lepers. Christ gravitated towards the least, the last and the lost.[9] No other religious leader did anything of the sort.[10]

Two: His Inherent Authority. The typical rabbi layered his message on top of those who had taught before him. Again, Jesus was different. He dismissed much of the "party line" as misguided folly. This was especially true of the "protective hedge" the Pharisees had built around God's law.[11] He even prefaced some of his remarks by saying, "You have heard it said …, but I say to you …." This was not only a challenge to what others were advocating, but to the collective mindset of the Pharisees in general. In doing so, Jesus asserted an authority all his own and placed it above the recognized teachers of the Law.

Three: His Miraculous Powers. Perhaps the biggest reason Christ drew crowds was his ability to heal the sick. Even more than turning water into wine, calming a storm, feeding 5,000 or raising the dead, Christ's ability to provide sight to the blind and sound to the deaf got their attention. Remember, this was a world before aspirin and antibiotics – that is, this was a world where the average life expectancy was thirty-five years and a simple fever might lead to death. Against that backdrop, the excitement created by Jesus's healing power is hard to overstate.

Three Years on the Road

Between his baptism by John and his final entry into Jerusalem, Christ spent three years traveling from village to village, preaching, teaching and healing the sick. We do not know as much about this time as we'd like, but we know enough to say several things. [12]

He Focused on Twelve Men. Shortly after his preaching tour began, Christ selected a dozen students to travel with him.[13] There was nothing particularly unusual about this. Rabbis had disciples. Jesus was a Rabbi, therefore, Jesus had disciples. But this group was different. For starters, they were not the most promising prospects. Secondly, unlike the disciples of other rabbis', they were not training in hopes of eventually replacing their Master. They simply wanted to be with him. Finally, there was also the size of the group. Jesus had a dozen disciples. The astute reader eventually realizes that this number is significant. Christ had selected twelve men because this group was symbolically replacing the twelve tribes of Israel as the pillars of God's work.

The Crowds Grew Large. Jesus quickly became one of the most popular teachers in Israel. In fact, he became a bit of a first century rock star. Luke describes one event where the surging crowds almost crushed him. Mark tells of men who destroyed a building just to get close to him, and Matthew numbers one gathering at over 10,000 people.[14] These crowds seldom play more than a supporting role in Christ's story – in fact, as the years unfold, Jesus spent less time with the masses and more time with the twelve.[15] But the crowds document his rock star status. During his thirty-six months on the road, Jesus became one of the most talked about people in the country.

He Gained Enemies. Not everyone who heard the "Son of Man" speak fell in love with him. In addition to his spellbound fans, Jesus acquired powerful enemies. This latter group eventually grew large enough to sway public opinion, force Pilate's hand and have Jesus killed. Those who confuse Christ with Mr. Rogers are usually surprised by this.[16] They cannot understand how a soft-spoken, self-effacing prophet-of-peace could end up mocked, whipped and crucified. Yet Christ was.

How did this happen? Why did people hate him?[17] Why would so many react so violently against a man whose main message was, "be nice?"

The answer is simple: his main message was something quite different.

Jesus did not act like the consummate Eagle Scout. He did not suggest that everyone be nice, play fair and use their inside voice. He challenged popular beliefs, spoke truth to power and made radical demands. He also unashamedly pointed to himself. Christ claimed to be radically different and better than everyone else.

In order to understand this, we need to take a closer look at what He said and did.

Jesus on Jesus

Though Christ lived simply and put the needs of others ahead of his own, he was not shy or self-effacing. He made cosmic claims about his nature, purpose and calling. He accepted worship and forgave sins. According to Jesus, he was God, Lord and Messiah. He was the eternal First Born Son who had arrived in humility, would die in ignominy and return in glorious power. Christ claimed that he would ultimately rule as the judge and sovereign king over the entire universe. Indeed, Christ claimed that he had created the universe. In ways big and small, Jesus announced that he was the center of the story and the focal point of history.

Consider just a few of his "I Am" statements:

- I am the door; if anyone enters through Me, he will be saved, and will go in and out and find pasture."

- I am the resurrection and the life; he who believes in Me will live even if he dies, and everyone who lives and believes in Me will never die.

- I am the bread of life; he who comes to Me will not hunger, and he who believes in Me will never thirst.

- I am the way, and the truth, and the life; no one comes to the Father but through Me. [18]

Do these sound like the views of a gentle and retiring man? Of course not, and they hardly stand alone.

When a Jewish leader asked Christ, "How do I gain eternal life?" Jesus simply pointed to himself. He did not suggest that the man pray, fast or tithe. He said, "For God so loved the world that he gave his only begotten son, that whoever believes in him – that is, in Me – shall not perish but have everlasting life."

When a Samaritan woman realized that Jesus was a prophet and started peppering him with religious questions, Christ cut through her confusion and told her exactly what she needed to know instead. It was him. He was the "living water" that would satisfy her true thirst.

Time after time, Jesus lay at the center of his own message. He claimed to be the God-Man sent to lay down his life as a sacrifice for the sins of the world.[19] More than teaching the Law, serving as an example, acting as a spiritual guide or reforming society, Jesus was born to die. His main message was not, "Keep these rules," but "believe in me."

Is it any wonder that the religious leaders who heard him speak ripped their clothes and pulled out their hair – the very things they were expected to do if they heard blasphemy? He was not suggesting minor modifications to their system, He was arguing that He fulfilled it. Christ taught that their Scriptures pointed to Him and that He was The One they had been waiting for.

Once Christ's claims come into focus, you will start to see them on every page. Of course, there is a big difference between saying you are God and actually being divine. Anyone can claim anything. As C.S. Lewis pointed out in his famous "tri-lemma," Jesus is either God, as he claims, or he is an evil liar trying to fool others, or he is simply delusional – he believes that he is God when he is not. You will have to decide what you believe about this. I suspect my position is pretty clear. However, at the moment I am simply trying to show that he did claim to be God.

To that end, let me highlight four other important texts where the real meaning of what was going on is frequently missed. [20]

One: His Sermon in Nazareth: Christ revealed more of his divine nature and purposes as he moved closer to the cross. But there is plenty to see at the beginning of his ministry if you know where to look. For instance, one of his first stops after becoming a rabbi was in his hometown of Nazareth. Luke records this visit in the fourth chapter of his Gospel. There he writes:

> Jesus went to Nazareth, where he had been brought up, and on the Sabbath day he went into the synagogue, as was his custom. He stood up to read, and the scroll of the prophet Isaiah was handed to him. Unrolling it, he found the place where it is written:
>
> > "The Spirit of the Lord is on me, because he has anointed me to proclaim good news to the poor. He has sent me to proclaim freedom for the prisoners and recovery of sight for the blind, to set the oppressed free, to proclaim the year of the Lord's favor."
>
> Then he rolled up the scroll, gave it back to the attendant and sat down. The eyes of everyone in the synagogue were fastened on him. He began by saying to them, "Today this scripture is fulfilled in your hearing."

It's unclear whether Christ selected the Isaiah passage himself or if it was the assigned reading of the day. What is clear is this: he claimed it was written about him. Jesus claimed that he was the one anointed to proclaim good news to the poor and freedom to the prisoner. He was the one sent to heal the blind and announce God's favor. Here – at the very beginning of his public ministry – Jesus claimed that a Messianic prophecy written 700 years before he was born, had been written to describe him. Christ was claiming to be the Messiah.[21]

Two - Debating the Pharisees: John 8 contains an extended interaction between Jesus and the Pharisees. It begins when he artfully dismantles a trap they set for him concerning a woman caught in adultery,[22] and then continues with a back and forth over his claims about himself. We pick up the conversation midstream in verse 48:

> The Jews answered him, "Aren't we right in saying that you are a Samaritan and demon-possessed?"
>
> "I am not possessed by a demon," said Jesus, "but I honor my Father and you dishonor me. I am not seeking glory for myself; but there is one who seeks it, and he is the judge. Very truly I tell you, whoever obeys my word will never see death."
>
> At this they exclaimed, "Now we know that you are demon-possessed! Abraham died and so did the prophets, yet you say that whoever obeys your word will never taste death. Are you greater than our father Abraham? He died, and so did the prophets. Who do you think you are?"
>
> Jesus replied, "If I glorify myself, my glory means nothing. My Father, whom you claim as your God, is the one who glorifies me. Though you do not know him, I know him. If I said I did not, I would be a liar like you, but I do know him and obey his word. Your father Abraham rejoiced at the thought of seeing my day; he saw it and was glad."
>
> "You are not yet fifty years old," they said to him, "and you have seen Abraham!"
>
> "Very truly I tell you," Jesus answered, "before Abraham was born, I am!" At this, they picked up stones to stone him, but Jesus hid himself, slipping away from the temple grounds.

There is a lot going on in this passage. I only wish to highlight one thing: Christ's use of the divine name – Yahweh or "I AM" – for himself. In order to appreciate how remarkable this was, I need to explain two things:

- **God's Name is Sacred:** God has many titles (Lord, Almighty, King, Sovereign, et al) but only one name (Yahweh, or, it's English translation, I AM.) He revealed this name to Moses shortly after calling him to lead the Jews out of slavery. Moses had responded with a question: "Suppose I go to the Israelites and say to them, 'The God of your fathers has sent me to you,' and they ask me, 'What is his name?' Then what shall I tell them?" God said to Moses, "I AM WHO I AM. This is what you are to say to the Israelites: 'I AM has sent me to you.'" I AM (which is also written in its un-translated form, Yahweh) is God's sacred name.

- **No One Said This Name:** First century Jews were very conscious of the sacredness of the Divine Name. In fact, because they believed that the second commandment forbid uttering it in a less than reverent way, most simply stopped saying it altogether. Hebrew scribes even stopped writing it. Whenever they came to the word Yahweh they wrote Lord instead.

In light of this you can imagine how shocking Christ's comments to the Pharisees are. In stating, "before Abraham was, I AM," Jesus was not simply claiming to be older and more important than Abraham, he was taking God's sacred name as his own.

The religious leaders who heard him say, "I AM" quickly forgot about the woman caught in adultery. Christ's offense was much worse, so they aimed their stones at him instead. Thankfully, he slipped away from them.

Three: Peter's Confession: Towards the end of Christ's public ministry, Matthew records Peter's moment of divine insight. It occurs shortly after Jesus and the disciples entered Caesarea Philippi and he asked them, "Who do people say the Son of Man is?"

"Some say John the Baptist; others say Elijah; and still others, Jeremiah or one of the prophets."

"But what about you?" he asked. "Who do you say I am?"

Simon Peter answered, "You are the Christ, the Son of the living God."

Those who have grown up hearing the words Jesus and Christ together miss the force of this exchange. Christ is not Jesus' last name,[23] it's the Greek term for Messiah, or "anointed one." When Peter declares, "You are the Christ," he is announcing that Jesus is no mere miracle worker, he is The One. Jesus is the "seed of woman," the heir promised to Abraham, the root of Jesse and the King who will sit on the throne of David forever.[24] He is the fulfillment of the Hebrew prophecies and the leader the entire nation has been waiting for. He is the Christ.[25]

And that is not all Peter said. His full reply went beyond, "You are the Christ," to include, "the Son of the Living God." In other words, Peter not only declared that Jesus was the Messiah, he also acknowledged that Christ was divine. This was new news.

The Jews had been looking for a political and military Messiah to overthrow the Romans and restore them to world power. They pictured someone a lot like King David. Peter's words declared that Jesus was more than that. He was God.

The rest of the Gospels make it clear that Peter did not fully understand what he was saying. But Christ did. In fact, Jesus celebrated Peter's reply, stating, "Blessed are you, Simon son of Jonah, for this was not revealed to you by flesh and blood, but by my Father in heaven." [26]

In other words, Jesus not only agreed with Peter's Confession, he attributed it to God Himself.

Four: The Transfiguration: The final moment I want to profile occurred one week later on the Mount of Transfiguration. All three of the Synoptic Gospels record this event. Matthew's account reads as follows:

After six days Jesus took with him Peter, James and John the brother of James, and led them up a high mountain by themselves. There he was transfigured before them. His face shone like the sun, and his clothes became as white as the light. Just then there appeared before them Moses and Elijah, talking with Jesus.

Peter said to Jesus, "Lord, it is good for us to be here. If you wish, I will put up three shelters—one for you, one for Moses and one for Elijah."
While he was still speaking, a bright cloud enveloped them, and a voice from the cloud said, "This is my Son, whom I love; with him I am well pleased. Listen to him!"

When the disciples heard this, they fell facedown to the ground, terrified. But Jesus came and touched them. "Get up," he said. "Don't be afraid." When they looked up, they saw no one except Jesus.
As they were coming down the mountain, Jesus instructed them, "Don't tell anyone what you have seen, until the Son of Man has been raised from the dead."

What exactly happened?[27] John 17 provides some insight. There we overhear Christ prayerfully asking the Father to, "glorify me in your presence with the glory I had with you before the world began" (emphasis mine).

Philippians 2 offers even more clarity. In that letter Paul celebrates Jesus' willingness to set aside the glory of heaven in order to serve others and die on the cross.[28] He describes Christ this way:

> Who, being in very nature God,
> did not consider equality with God something to be grasped,
> but made himself nothing,
> taking the very nature of a servant,
> being made in human likeness.
> And being found in appearance as a man,
> he humbled himself
> by becoming obedient to death—
> even death on a cross!

The key line for us is the third one: but made himself nothing. The New American Standard Version of the Bible reads, "he emptied himself."
The King James edition says he, "made himself of no reputation." When translations vary this much, it usually means the perfect word does not exist. In this case, the problem is a little different. The truth is, we do not know how to describe what happened because we do not really understand what happened. A clear grasp of God's nature is beyond our comprehension.

We know that Jesus existed as God before the creation of the world. We know that at the incarnation he added humanity to deity, and we know that this "addition" required him to hold back aspects of himself in some way. Hundreds of books, thousands of articles and tens of thousands of sermons have speculated on exactly what Christ "placed on hold" in order to maintain the unity of two natures – one divine and one human – in himself.[29] We may never be able to understand it. But this much is clear. Matthew's report on the Transfiguration shows that for a few brief moments whatever Christ had set aside was made visible to Peter, James and John.[30] The veil covering his glory was lifted and they saw his face "shining like the sun."

There is More, But...

We could continue to build the case that Christ is both God and the Messiah. If we turned to the Old Testament we could document how perfectly Jesus fulfilled the Messianic prophecies,[31] and show how many of the titles ascribed to Him were previously used to describe the Father.

If we included the Book of Acts, we could show how quickly everyone began to testify to the "supremacy, dignity, majesty and god-ness of Christ.[32] And if we included the Epistles we could list hundreds of instances where Jesus is referred to in ways that people only speak of God.

There is much more. But it's time to draw this chapter to a close.

For the record, neither Christ's claim to be God, nor the related testimony of those closest to him prove that he is divine. But I hope this much is clear: this is the Bible's main message. Both the Old and New Testaments point in the same direction – Jesus is the Messiah and Son of God. He once was only God. At the incarnation He added humanity to deity. He did this in part to reveal God's nature, serve as an example and fulfill prophecy. But the chief reason he did this was in order to die in our place.

Christ is the rescuer. And the plan set in place since the beginning reaches its climax as he enters Jerusalem for the Passover.

The Least You Can Know

In the next chapter we will focus on the final week of Christ's life. This includes his betrayal, arrest, trial, scourging, crucifixion, death and burial. But before we do, it is important to be clear about what we have learned.

- The Gospels present Jesus as a miracle worker who gathered crowds, taught with authority and challenged the views of Judea's religious leaders.

- He began his public ministry after he was baptized by John the Baptist and successfully withstood the temptations of Satan.

- His public ministry spanned about three years. During that time he traveled throughout Judea with his disciples, preaching, teaching and healing.

- He drew crowds because of his love, authority and supernatural power. He made enemies, particularly among the religious authorities, for his bold claims about his nature and purpose.

- The ultimate focus of Christ's teaching was Christ himself. He claimed to be the Messiah sent from God to save people from their sins. This claim was veiled at first, but grew clearer over time.

ENDNOTES

[1] During a Passover Seder – the meal that stands in the center of the holiday – Jewish families set a place at the table for Elijah. At some point during the meal, the youngest child is expected to open the front door and look to see if he is coming to join them. They do this to acknowledge that his arrival is the next thing they are expecting. Elijah must return before the Messiah arrives.

[2] God used three different offices to govern the nation of Israel: 1) Kings were anointed to oversee civil and military affairs; 2) Priests were required to represent the people to God (chiefly by offering sacrifices in the temple); and 3) Prophets were expected to represent God to the people. If the people

were being obedient, kings and priests were enough. Generally speaking, it was only when more help was needed that prophets were called on to "foretell" or "forth-tell" God's message. The role was generally filled by quirky men who lived solitary lives, often in the desert. They seldom were called upon to deliver good news. And between the odd way they were expected to deliver the message (e.g., Ezekiel was forced to lay on his side for 399 days, Hosea was told to marry a prostitute) and the way they were treated by those they spoke to (e.g., Jeremiah was lowered into a well, Isaiah was cut in half, John the Baptist was beheaded, etc.) it was a difficult life. Being a prophet was not a job you aspired to.

[3] Matthew 3:1-12, esp. 9

[4] Luke 3:7-8. The Pharisees believed that when the Messiah came he would overthrow Rome, return Israel to power and vindicate their righteousness. After all, they were the true heirs of Abraham. John the Baptist told them that their self-righteousness lay at the base of their problems and that God could raise up descendants of Abraham from the stones if he needed to.

[5] Talk of Satan may cause some to wince, especially those who mistakenly picture him in a red spandex body suit, complete with horns and a tail. The Bible does not describe him this way. But it does recognize evil as real and speaks at some length about "spiritual forces of darkness," which are led by a fallen angel.

[6] The "Testing of Jesus" in the wilderness closely parallels Adam's testing in the Garden of Eden. Of course there are differences: 1) Adam had a companion while Christ was alone; 2) Adam was in a garden paradise while Christ was in a desert wilderness; 3) Adam's needs were met while Christ was weak from a 40 day fast; and, of course, 4) Adam failed – and in him all of humanity fell as well – whereas Christ passed the test and provided a way of reconciliation for all who follow him. But the Apostle Paul makes much of the similarities, going so far as to call Jesus the "Second Adam" and arguing that both Adam and Jesus took the test as representatives for the rest of humanity. Volumes have been written about this high-stakes encounter. Theologians discuss the nature of Satan's offers, the Old Testament passages Christ used in his defense, and what might have happened if Jesus had failed. A simple reading suggests that little of what Satan encouraged Christ to do was inherently wrong. For example, Satan told Christ to turn stones into bread. Jesus refused, but later multiplied the bread to feed the five thousand. If Satan's requests were not wrong in themselves then why did Christ reject them? Because: 1) they were designed to honor Satan; and 2) they suggested that Christ's mission might be accomplished without the cross. The New Testament suggests that Jesus continued towards Golgotha in obedience to the Father and for our redemption. And, in spite of the

additional obstacles he faced, he remained perfectly righteous. Christ made it through life without sin.

[7] Luke 4:12

[8] Rabbinical students were expected to: 1) master both the content and delivery of their rabbi's teaching; 2) help with simple chores; and 3) learn how to do every aspect of the job. This apprenticeship lasted more than a dozen years. Those who successfully completed it became rabbis when they turned thirty.

[9] Jewish scholar Geza Vermes says that Christ's association with the "misfits of Palestinian society" was one of his most revolutionary acts, and that it not only drew hostile criticism, but it distinguished him from both his contemporaries and his predecessors. "The prophets spoke on behalf of the honest poor and defended the widows and fatherless, those oppressed and exploited by the wicked, the rich and the powerful. Jesus went further. In addition to proclaiming these blessed, he actually took his stand among the pariahs of his world, those despised by the respectable. Sinners were his table companions and the ostracized tax collectors and prostitutes were his friends." (Geze Vermes, Jesus the Jew (London: Collins, 1973), p. 224. Cited by Vinoth Ramachandra in The Scandal of Jesus, IVP, 2001, p. 8f).

[10] This is not to suggest that Christ ignored those with money and power. A careful reading of the Gospels makes it clear that he did not. He accepted dinner invitations from the "haves" as well as the "have-nots." He even spent time with Romans and Pharisees. But it's also clear that his default approach was to focus on those others avoided.

[11] In an effort to prevent anyone from breaking God's laws, the Pharisees established a ring of laws around God's law. This "protective hedge" ensured that you didn't even get close to breaking God's laws. For example, Exodus 23:19 prohibits cooking a baby goat in its mother's milk. A "hedge" around this law eventually became the requirement to keep a "Kosher kitchen" – i.e., to maintain two separate sets of cooking utensils, one for dairy products and the other for non-dairy cooking. This prevented you from accidentally having a minute portion of milk in a pot used to cook the meat of a young goat.

[12] We know more about what Christ did during the three years he spent with the disciples than we do about any other time in his life, but even here we do not know much. One third of the Synoptic Gospels and one half of the Gospel of John are dedicated to the last week of Christ's life. When you realize that most of the rest of their pages are taken up recording what he said – his sermons, parables and other teachings – you realize how little

space is dedicated to what he did. John ends his Gospel stating, "Jesus did many other things as well. If every one of them were written down, I suppose that even the whole world would not have room for the books that would be written." Given the choice between "more books and less space" or "less books and more space" most of us would give up the space! (At least we think we would. We actually have a hard time dealing with what we do have!). Perhaps in heaven all of Christ's work will be on display and we can fill in all the gaps.

[13] Alongside the disciples there were others, including a group of women who appear to be the ones financing much of the costs incurred by Christ and the twelve. This larger group often traveled from town to town with Jesus.

[14] In Matthew 14:2, Matthew reports that there were "about five thousand men, besides women and children." Most scholars assume that this meant that in addition to 5,000 men, there were another 5,000 women plus several thousand children. There were other indications that the crowds were large as well. In Jericho, Zacchaeus was forced to climb a tree to see Jesus. In Mark 3 we are told that so many people were trying to hear him teach from his spot on the beach that he had his disciples had to get a boat ready so he could move into the bay.

[15] They were attracted by his wisdom and power, but as he spent less time healing the sick and more time talking about the cost of following him, those who were there for the free food moved on.

[16] If I've hopelessly dated myself by referring to Mr. Rogers, let me simply note that he was a staple of children's TV for about thirty years, and famously known as a mild, smiling, happy and perfectly harmless man.

[17] People grew angry with Christ for several different reasons – some got mad when Jesus would not give them what they asked for. Others were upset over his interpretation of the law. The Scribes and Pharisees seethed because he called them names – e.g., "white washed tombs," "children of the devil" and "snake handlers" – undermined their teaching and dismissed their nationalism. But the issue that led to his death was Christ's claim to be God.

[18] The "I am" passages are found in John 6:35; 8:12; 8:23; 10:7-9, 14-15; 11:25.

[19] When Jesus was asked why he came he responded, "The Son of Man did not come to be served but to be serve, and to lay down his life a ransom for many." Matthew 20:28f

[20] In a longer study we could additionally unpack: 1) His first miracle in Cana; 2) the time he calmed the storm in Galilee; 3) the raising of Lazarus from the dead and a dozen other moments.

[21] It appears to have taken a while for those in the synagogue to grasp what Jesus was saying. The congregation's initial response was friendly. Luke reports that, "all spoke well of him and marveled at the gracious words coming out of his mouth." But their reaction grew cooler as Jesus continued to talk, and as they had time to think about what he was saying. Before long they grew hostile. Eventually they grabbed Christ and carried him to a cliff to throw him to his death. Jesus was somehow able to walk away from the mob and leave the area. He would never visit Nazareth again, but he would make the claim to be the Messiah with greater force and clarity in the weeks and months ahead.

[22] In John 8:1-11, the Pharisees bring a woman caught in the act of adultery to Jesus. They remind him that the Law of Moses calls for her to be stoned and then ask what he recommends. If he says that she should be let go, they will seek to discredit him as a teacher of the Law. But if he says to stone her, he would likely be arrested by the Romans for illegally issuing the death penalty. Jesus brilliantly turns their trap on them by responding, "Let he who is without sin cast the first stone." He then forgives the woman, telling her to go and sin no more.

[23] In commenting on the prominence of the term Christ – which means Messiah - Justo Gonzalez writes: This was such an important element in their proclamation, that very soon they became known as "Christians," that is, followers or servants of the Christos. According to Acts, this new name was first given to them in Antioch, where some Jewish followers of the new sect – what Acts calls "the way" – began preaching to the Gentiles. As a result, it became customary for Christians to speak of their Savior as "Jesus Christ" – Jesus the anointed. Very soon what had originally been an adjective or participle, "Christ," became a name, so that people began referring to Jesus simply as "Christ." (Gonzalez, p. 112).

[24] Speaking through Nathan, God promised David that his kingdom would endure forever. This prophecy is found in 2 Samuel 7:11b: "'The LORD declares to you that the LORD himself will establish a house for you: When your days are over and you rest with your fathers, I will raise up your offspring to succeed you, who will come from your own body, and I will establish his kingdom. He is the one who will build a house for my Name, and I will establish the throne of his kingdom forever. I will be his father, and he will be my son."

[25] As has been noted several times, the Jews were expecting the Messiah to

be a political and/or military leader. They not only did not expect a Savior, they were not expecting the Savior to be divine. Peter's declaration that Jesus is not simply the Anointed One, but also God, was not only a turning point, it was a double confession.

[26] Matthew 16:14ff

[27] I am referencing Christ's Transfiguration to show that his true nature was glorious. For the record, the passage also elevates Christ by placing him above Moses and Elijah. The first represented the Law and the second the Prophets. This passage makes it clear that they were not Christ's equals. They were servants, Jesus is the Son. Peter foolishly suggested that three altars be built. God the Father prevents Peter from making any other inane comments by praising Jesus, announcing, "This is my Son, whom I love; with him I am well pleased. Listen to him!"

[28] The passage being quoted here is an early hymn that Paul inserts into his letter.

[29] Theologians refer to Christ's dual nature (God and Man) as the hypostatic union. It is a mystery every bit as profound as the Trinity, and as such, lies beyond our full comprehension. For a longer treatment of the Hypostatic Union see the Chalcedonian Definition, one of the church's earliest creeds.

[30] In the days following Peter's confession, Jesus had started talking about his upcoming death and resurrection. He had explained that he was going to suffer, be "rejected by the elders, chief priests and teachers of the law," and killed before being raised back to life on the third day. Luke explains that Christ also spoke about the high cost of following him, saying: "If anyone would come after me, he must deny himself and take up his cross daily and follow me. For whoever wants to save his life will lose it, but whoever loses his life for me will save it." It is hard to know exactly what the twelve were thinking at this time. (One moment Jesus is confirming that he is the Messiah and promising to launch a kingdom that will prevail against all foes, the next minute he says he is going to die.) But it seems likely that they knew they were in danger. It was not unusual for a revolutionary's lieutenants to be killed at the same time the leader was. It's hard to believe they were oblivious to that. Perhaps Christ's Transfiguration happened in part to keep them from walking away. Whatever the case, two things are clear: Christ ended his statements about the challenges ahead of them with a promise that some of them would see the kingdom of God come with power; and the very next words in Mark's Gospel describe Christ in his true glory.

[31] Examples of some of the Messianic prophecies fulfilled by Christ include:

he would be born in Bethlehem; he would be born to a virgin; he would be a descendent of David; he would grow up in Nazareth; he would suffer and die; he would be buried in a rich man's tomb, etc. (Note: all of these were made hundreds of years before he was born and most lay outside his ability to manipulate).

[32] As John Proctor notes, a broad body of material – creeds poems, sermons and the like – was developed in Jerusalem and elsewhere, all testifying to the "supremacy, dignity, majesty and god-ness of Christ." (John Proctor, First Impression, Dec. 2009).

74

CHAPTER 4
The Lamb of God - From the Parade to the Cross

Christianity, if false, is of no importance, and if true, of infinite importance. The only thing it cannot be is moderately important.
C.S. Lewis

I am enthralled by the luminous figure of the Nazarene. Jesus is too colossal for the pen of the phrase-mongers, however artful...No one can read the gospels without feeling the actual presence of Jesus. His personality pulsates in every word. No myth is filled with such life.
Albert Einstein

Amazing Love! How can it be, That Thou, My God, shouldst die for me?
Charles Wesley

Six days remain.

We've traced Christ's life from 'before creation' through his final journey towards Jerusalem. It's time to enter the city for Holy Week, a tumultuous series of events that begin with his Triumphal Entry and cascade down to his crucifixion.

Many people skip over Holy Week. They move right from Palm Sunday to Easter without thinking much about what happened in between. The Gospel writers do not. They slow down. Matthew, Mark and Luke devote one-third of their accounts to these six days. John devotes half.[1] Clearly, the 144 hours between Christ's entrance into Jerusalem and his crucifixion outside its gates, are enormously important. In many ways, everything that precedes them is prelude and everything that follows is postlude. Holy Week is the pivot point of history.

By way of review, let me note that Jesus is now a major figure in Palestine – famous in some circles, infamous in others, but known by virtually everyone. Also he has become increasingly vocal about two things: he is God, and he is heading into Jerusalem to be killed.[2] His disciples have some understanding of the first point, but virtually no appreciation of the second. Peter has even tried to stop Christ from talking about his death. But Jesus is adamant. He knew he would die in Jerusalem. Indeed, that is why he was headed there. He had come "to give his life as a ransom for many" and Israel's capital was the place he intended to do it. [3]

As in our earlier studies, we will do our best to take the events of Holy Week in chronological order.[4] But before we enter the city there are two matters that require a bit of explanation: the Passover Festival and the politics of Judea.

The Passover Festival

Jesus timed his march into Jerusalem to coincide with the annual Passover Festival. We need to understand why.

The First Passover: As you may know, the last chapters of Genesis report that a famine forced Jacob, his sons and their families to leave the Promised Land around 1500 BC and settle in Egypt. They initially resided there as honored guests, but over time they fell from favor and were pressed into slavery. For 400 years they suffered under the hot Egyptian sun. Eventually God answered their cries and sent Moses to lead them to freedom.

After Moses' efforts to talk Pharaoh into releasing the Jews failed, God cursed Egypt with a series of plagues. The tenth and final was the worst – an angel of death swept over the land, claiming the life of the oldest male child in every family. To avoid losing their own first-born sons, God instructed the Jews to take the following steps:

> ...each man is to take a lamb for his family, one for each household. The animals you choose must be year-old males without defect. On the fourteenth day of the month, all the members of the community of Israel must slaughter them at twilight. Then they are to take some of the blood and put it on the sides and tops of the doorframes of the houses where they eat the lambs. That same night they are to eat the meat roasted over the fire, along with bitter herbs, and bread made without yeast. This is how you are to eat it: with your cloak tucked into your belt, your sandals on your feet and your staff in your hand.

Eat it in haste; it is the LORD's Passover.

On that same night I will pass through Egypt and strike down every firstborn of both people and animals, and I will bring judgment on all the gods of Egypt. I am the LORD. The blood will be a sign for you on the houses where you are, and when I see the blood, I will pass over you. No destructive plague will touch you when I strike Egypt.[5]

Because the Jews obeyed God's directive, the Angel of Death "passed over" their homes, and in the chaos that followed they were allowed to leave Egypt.

The Annual Festival: In addition to directing the Jews to paint their doorframes with lambs' blood, God also instructed them to memorialize the day. In Exodus 12:14 we read:

This is a day you are to commemorate; for the generations to come you shall celebrate it as a festival to the Lord – a lasting ordinance.

In obedience to this directive, the Jews annually gathered in Jerusalem for a Passover Festival. Christ made his triumphal entry into the city just as the festival was beginning. This was not by chance. Christ timed his arrival to reinforce his claim to be the true Passover sacrifice – the perfect, innocent, male lamb sent to die in order to take away the sins of the world.

I realize that this might catch you by surprise. In fact, if you've not made this connection before it can seem like quite a reach. Let me assure you, it's not. The entire Bible builds to this point. This will become clearer when we look at the Last Supper in just a few pages, but let me highlight a few points right now.

- God had been preparing his people for Christ's crucifixion since the first pages of Genesis. He did so in many ways. Perhaps the main one was the development of a sacrificial system that continually reinforced two critical tenets. The first is that sin is a capital offense – when we sin we deserve to die. The second is that substitute deaths are allowed – an innocent third party can die so that guilty people can go free.

- According to God's instructions, the Passover Lamb was to be a young male, without blemish, selected five days before it was killed, and put to death at three o'clock in the afternoon of the day before the Sabbath. Jesus was the perfect and blameless man. He entered Jerusalem five days before his death and was crucified at three o'clock on the day before the Sabbath. [7]

- Those slaughtering the lamb were under strict instructions not to break any of the animal's bones. Likewise, though it was common to break the legs of those being crucified – and though both of the men being crucified alongside Christ had their legs broken – Jesus' legs were left intact.[8]

There is more, such as John the Baptist's response when he saw Christ walking out to be baptized, "Behold the Lamb of God who takes away the sins of the world." Suffice it to say, the biblical writers do not merely claim that Christ leveraged the Passover in order to make a point. They claim that he fulfilled it. That is, they claim that the Passover was always about him. The blood of animals had never been sufficient to take away the sins of men,[9] the sacrifices were only pointing forward to the one whose blood actually would. Christ entered Jerusalem at the time of the Passover Festival because he was the Passover Lamb.

The Politics of Judea

The second bit of background information we need to review centers on the politics of Judea. Here there are three matters to highlight.

The Romans ruled the known world. At the time of Christ's death, Tiberius Caesar sat on the throne in Rome, governing the Empire through a network of kings, governors and generals. The province of Judea – that part of the Empire that included Jerusalem – was controlled by two of his appointments: a Roman governor named Pilate, and a "Jewish" king named Herod the Great. The Jews hated everything about this situation and longed for someone to lead them in a successful revolt against the Romans. In fact, they believed God had promised to send just such a person, a "messiah" molded in the image of David, the warrior king.

The situation was tense. Things were seldom calm in Judea, but they were particularly unstable during the Festival when 200,000 Jewish nationalists flooded into Jerusalem to celebrate their version of the Fourth of July.[10] If someone was looking for the opportune time to stage a coup d'état, the Passover was it. Pilate realized this; therefore he always spent the Festival in Jerusalem.[11]

Jesus was the man of the hour. John not only reports that many of those arriving for the Passover, "were curious about Jesus," he later adds two other points. First, Christ was the principal topic of conversation at the Temple, where people were asking each other, "What do you think? Will he show up at the Feast or not?"[12]   Secondly, it wasn't just the common person who was expressing interest in Christ. "The high priests and Pharisees gave out the word that anyone getting wind of him should inform them. They were all set to arrest him." Clearly, if first century Palestine had an Internet, Jesus would have gone viral.

With this backdrop in place, we are ready for the events of Holy Week, the pivot point of the Bible and human history. The long crescendo – which had started in Genesis 3, and was reinforced by the promises of the prophets and the blood of the sacrifices – was approaching a climax. Everything was pointing to Jesus, and Jesus was pointing to the cross.

Sunday - The Triumphal Entry

In order to find a place to stay and complete the pre-Passover rites of purification, those living outside Jerusalem generally arrived a few days before the festival started. With this in mind, Jesus and his disciples left Jericho and began walking towards the capital.

Given how many people were pouring into the city, it's quite possible that Christ might have been able to slip in unnoticed, but this was not the plan.[13] The time for caution was over. Jesus was ready to die, and Jerusalem was the place where he intended to do it. To that end the travel party stopped at the Mount of Olives so Christ could prepare for a grand entrance.

In Mark's Gospel we are told that Jesus sent two of his disciples to a village, saying:

"...as you enter it, you will find a colt tied there, which no one has ever ridden. Untie it and bring it here. If anyone asks you, 'Why are you doing this?' say, 'The Lord needs it and will send it back here shortly.'"

Luke reports that as soon as Christ began riding the donkey colt towards Jerusalem the people began to cheer. Matthew adds that "the whole city was stirred."

Modern readers may wonder how a donkey ride qualifies as a grand entrance. Christ's first-century contemporaries understood. One thousand years earlier, King Solomon had ridden a donkey into Jerusalem during his coronation parade. Several hundred years later, Zechariah prophesied that the Messiah would do the same.

> Rejoice greatly, Daughter Zion!
> Shout, Daughter Jerusalem!
> See, your king comes to you, righteous and victorious,
> Lowly and riding on a donkey, on a colt, the foal of a donkey. [14]

The burro was a perfect choice. It was understated – just like its rider – but it allowed Jesus to make a bold claim to Kingship. The crowd understood exactly what he was doing and responded by shouting "Hosanna" and waving palm branches, the first century equivalent of a Jewish flag.[15]

Christ's entrance into the city was everything the Roman authorities feared it might be. He had edged the crowd towards revolt just by riding into town. Clearly, they would respond to any call he issued. Remarkably, what Christ did next was even more provocative. But it went unnoticed by the Romans. This time it was the Jewish leaders' turn to be nervous.

Monday - Cleansing the Temple

On the morning after he paraded into the city, Jesus walked into the temple's outer court, took out a whip and proceeded to disrupt everyone and everything. He turned over the tables of the money changers and drove away the animals being sold as temple sacrifices.[16] When the officials asked him why he was doing all this, he replied, "Destroy this temple and in three days I will rebuild it." In order to appreciate just how confusing and unsettling his remarks were, you need to understand a few things about the Temple itself.

The Temple stood at the center of Jewish life. For first century Jews, the temple was the most important site in the world. It was their place of worship, center of culture and seat of government. Few countries have anything close to its equivalent. In the United States you would have to combine the White House, Pentagon, Wall Street, Lincoln Memorial and National Cathedral to even come close.

The Temple was the most holy place on earth. Though the Jews did not believe that God could be contained in a building, they did believe that he manifested his presence in the temple's inner sanctum – the Holy of Holies. This was the nexus of heaven and earth, the most sacred, valuable and holy piece of real estate in the universe.

It was vast and spectacularly beautiful. The courtyards Christ disrupted were part of the Second Temple. The first was constructed during Solomon's reign nearly one thousand years earlier. Tens of thousands of men worked for seven years to build the First Temple, completing it in 953 BC. and dedicating it in a lavish ceremony that included the slaughter of 22,000 oxen and 120,000 sheep.[17] Sacrifices took place at its altar for close to 400 years before it was destroyed by the Babylonians in 586 BC.

The Second Temple unfolded in two stages. A modest building was constructed under Zerubbabel's leadership shortly after a remnant of Jews returned from Babylonian exile. It was completed in 515 BC and used on a daily basis for the next 496 years.[18] In 19 BC, Herod the Great set out to dramatically expand it.[19] Once again, tens of thousands of men were pressed into service, but this time they labored for close to sixty years. The result was a complex so massive that it filled nearly one-quarter of the city of Jerusalem, and so spectacular that a first century historian described it this way:

> Viewed from without, the Sanctuary had everything that could amaze
> either mind or eyes. Overlaid all round with stout plates of gold,
> the first rays of the sun it reflected so fierce a blaze of fire that those

who endeavored to look at it were forced to turn away as if they had looked straight at the sun. To strangers as they approached it seemed in the distance like a mountain covered with snow; for any part not covered with gold was dazzling white... [20]

The Second Temple was not fully remodeled when Christ walked into its outer courtyard that Monday morning, but it was getting close. Ten thousand men had been working on it for forty-six years. [21]

It is unclear whether Jesus was upset because the money changers had set up shop inside the temple courts, because of the exorbitant exchange rates they were charging or both. Whatever the case, it was not just his actions that got their attention. They were also shocked by his reply to their question. When they asked, "What gives you the right to do this?" Jesus answered, "Destroy this temple and in three days I will raise it up." Not only was this not an answer to their question, it was unthinkable. Why would a Jew ever say such a thing? And beyond that, who could imagine rebuilding it in three days if it were destroyed? At least 10,000 men had been working on it for close to fifty years and they still were not done.

Why did Jesus make such an outlandish statement? The answer is simple. The Rabbi from Nazareth was making another bold claim. When Christ said, "Destroy this temple and in three days I will rebuild it," he was not talking about the building Herod was remodeling. He was talking about his own body. He was the temple. Jesus was claiming that as the God-Man he – not the building – was the ultimate intersection of divinity and humanity.[22] People no longer needed to go to a holy place to get close to God. All they needed to do was get close to him. And when he suggested that he'd raise the temple back up in three days, he was not speaking about rebuilding a structure; he was talking about his upcoming resurrection from the dead.

It is hard to overstate Christ's claims. He was not only suggesting that he was the Passover Lamb, he was arguing that he was the true temple and the end of the entire sacrificial system.

Tuesday and Wednesday

We are not given as much information about Tuesday and Wednesday as we are about Monday, but we are given enough to know that Jesus used the time to preach, debate, heal and otherwise draw increasing amounts of attention to himself.

We also know that during this time he sharpened his attacks against the Scribes and Pharisees. He criticized them for their pride and warned them that prostitutes and tax collectors were closer to God than they were, He called them all sorts of disparaging names, such as blind guides, fools, hypocrites and snakes.

They responded by plotting to end his life. During an emergency session of the Sanhedrin, Caiaphas, the high priest, argued that if Jesus stirred further unrest, Rome would step in and strip the Jews of the few freedoms they had left.[23] He went on to claim that it was better for "one man to die for the people" than for the whole nation to perish. Matthew reports that from that day on, "they plotted to take his life."[24]

It was also during this time that Judas agreed to betray Jesus for thirty pieces of silver. Some believe he grew frustrated with Christ's refusal to set up a worldly kingdom. Others argue that as the only one of the twelve who was not from Galilee he simply never fit in. Whatever the case, it was during one of these two days that Judas slipped away from the others and cut a deal with the authorities. In exchange for a pocketful of silver, Judas agreed to take them to where Christ was staying.

Thursday Evening - The Last Supper

On Thursday evening, Jesus and the disciples gathered in a private room for the Passover meal,[25] the special dinner that had been celebrated annually for 1,500 years.[26] The disciples knew the format well: bitter herbs were used to remind them of the harshness of Egyptian slavery, salt water was sipped to remind them of their ancestors' tears, unleavened bread was served to highlight how rushed the flight from Egypt had been, and four different cups of wine were poured to remind them of different aspects of God's promises.

Of course, the focal point of the meal was the Lamb. In keeping with tradition it had been sacrificed at the Temple earlier that day and then roasted whole. It was prominently featured to remind everyone that the Angel of Death had "passed over" their ancestors because the lambs' blood smeared over their doorframe indicated that their debt had already been atoned.

As I noted earlier, the format of the meal was well known to every Jew, including the disciples. They knew exactly how the meal was supposed to proceed. Consequently they would have paid close attention when Christ veered from the script and started directing everything towards himself. Matthew reports that:

During the meal Jesus took the bread, and when he had given thanks, he broke it and gave it to his disciples, saying, "Take and eat; this is my body." Then he took a cup, and when he had given thanks, he gave it to them, saying, "Drink from it, all of you. This is my blood of the covenant, which is poured out for many for the forgiveness of sins. I tell you, I will not drink from this fruit of the vine from now on until that day when I drink it new with you in my Father's kingdom."

It's hard to know what the disciples thought about the meal. It's not until after the resurrection that they begin to understand what Christ was saying and doing. But it's very clear to those of us who have had time to reflect on his words, especially in light of the teaching found in the rest of the New Testament. Jesus was pointing to himself once again. He was claiming to be the focal point of God's plan. He was announcing that the lamb was no longer necessary. In fact, it had always been only a placeholder waiting for Christ's death. Jesus was claiming that He was the ultimate sacrifice, the true Paschal Lamb, the "suffering servant" sent to take away the sins of the world.

Thursday Night - The Garden of Gethsemane

Following the meal, Jesus and his disciples left the upper room, walked through the city gates, crossed the Kidron Valley and climbed the Mount of Olives. There, in an orchard called Gethsemane, they sat down to rest. Jesus was tormented by what he knew awaited him, so he asked the three men he was closest to – Peter, James and John – for their support. "My soul is overwhelmed with sorrow to the point of death," he said to them. "Stay here and keep watch with me." Going a little farther, he fell with his face to the ground and prayed, "My Father, if it is possible, may this cup be taken from me. Yet not as I will, but as you will."

On several occasions Jesus returned to his three disciples for encouragement, but each time he found them asleep. Finally, in the early morning hours, he woke them to announce:

> "It is time....The hour has come. Look, the Son of Man is betrayed into the hands of sinners. Rise! Let us go! Here comes my betrayer!"[28]

At that moment, Judas led a group of armed men right to Jesus. At least one of the disciples drew a sword to defend Christ, but Jesus quickly made it clear that he intended to go peacefully.

> "Am I leading a rebellion that you have come out with swords and clubs to capture me? Every day I was with you, teaching in the temple courts, and you did not arrest me. But the Scriptures must be fulfilled." Then everyone deserted him and fled.[29]

Christ had not come to Jerusalem to fight his enemies. He had come to die for them. And so, as his followers scattered, Jesus was led back to Jerusalem to face charges. In less than twelve hours he would be dead.

Friday - The Trial(s)

It's common to refer to "the trial" of Jesus as if there were only one, and to assume that an impartial jury actually objectively examined evidence before rendering a verdict. That is not what happened. Instead, Christ was paraded before a number of groups, most of whom had already decided on both his guilt and punishment.

Annas: Annas was the first to question Jesus. As the former high priest, his assignment was to learn as much as he could in order to coach the rest of the Sanhedrin on how to proceed. But Christ refused to talk to Annas, so eventually Jesus was sent directly to the full council.

The Sanhedrin: The seventy priests, scribes and elders who served on this council received Christ in the early morning hours. A number of witnesses were brought before them to testify against Jesus, but their stories did not line up, and for a while it appeared as though they would be unable to proceed. Caiaphas, the high priest, eventually broke the impasse by questioning Jesus directly. Referring to the charges being leveled against him, Caiaphas asked:

> "Are you not going to answer? What is this testimony that these men are bringing against you?" But Jesus remained silent and gave no answer.

> Again the high priest asked him, "Are you the Messiah, the Son of the Blessed One?"

> "I am," said Jesus. "And you will see the Son of Man sitting at the right hand of the Mighty One and coming on the clouds of heaven."

> The high priest tore his clothes.[30] "Why do we need any more witnesses?" he asked. "You have heard the blasphemy. What do you think?"[31]

Many mistakenly imagine that Christ used the title "Son of Man" as a gesture of humility. Instead of referring to himself as the "Son of God," "Savior," "Messiah" or something more forceful, he referred to himself as the "Son of Man." Those more familiar with the title knew better. "Son of Man" was a bit obscure, but it was a very bold claim to divinity. In Daniel 7 it is used to describe one equal with God the Father. There we read:

> In my vision at night I looked, and there before me was one like a son of man, coming with the clouds of heaven. He approached the Ancient of Days and was led into his presence. He was given authority, glory and sovereign power; all nations and peoples of every language worshiped him. His dominion is an everlasting dominion that will not pass away, and his kingdom is one that will never be destroyed.

Claiming to be the Son of Man was one of the boldest things Christ could do. In taking this title as his own he was not only claiming to be the

Messiah, he was also claiming to be fully divine. Furthermore, he was announcing that he would eventually sit at the right hand of the Father and exercise dominion over everyone and everything.

This was more than the members of the Sanhedrin could allow. Some started beating him. Others spit in his face. Had they enjoyed the legal authority to put him to death, they almost certainly would have stoned him right then. But Rome had not granted them that power, so they sent him to Pilate instead.

Pilate: The Sanhedrin would have avoided Pilate if they could have, for the Roman governor was not only unpredictable, he seemed to delight in not doing what they asked. Furthermore, although he was quick to order people to their death, he was unlikely to be bothered by Christ's claims to be God. (The Romans already had one million gods. What was one more?) Unfortunately, there was no way to avoid the governor. He was in town specifically for situations such as this, and he was the only one who could order Christ killed. So, they highlighted Christ's claims to be king and sent Jesus to Pilate, demanding that the governor deal with this threat to Caesar and treason against Rome.

Luke wrote:

> Then the whole assembly rose and led him off to Pilate. And they began to accuse him, saying, "We have found this man subverting our nation. He opposes payment of taxes to Caesar and claims to be Messiah, a king."[33]

Pilate questioned Jesus two times. After the first round he was inclined to let Christ go – a move his wife was encouraging as well[34] -- but he could not afford to appear weak. Jesus was a destabilizing force. And now Christ was being portrayed as a rival to Caesar and a threat to the Empire – these were charges the governor could not ignore. Pilate bought a bit of time by sending Jesus to Herod Antipas, the governor of Galilee. And he questioned him a second time before going to the people and offering to release Jesus in honor of the Passover. But the chief priest and other authorities appear to have anticipated this, and had "stirred up" the crowd to demand the release of Barabbas, a career criminal, instead.

They also filled the courtyard outside Pilate's home with cries for Christ's execution. [35]

> Pilate held out a bit longer. In fact, he went back to the crowd three times suggesting that there was no good reason to have Jesus killed. The last time he offered to have him flogged before releasing him, but the cries for Christ's crucifixion only grew. Eventually he relented.

> Pilate said to them, "Then what should I do with Jesus who is called the Christ?" They all said, "Crucify him!" He asked, "Why? What wrong has he done?" But they shouted more insistently, "Crucify him!" When Pilate saw that he could do nothing, but that instead a riot was starting, he took some water, washed his hands before the crowd and said, "I am innocent of this man's blood. You take care of it yourselves!" In reply all the people said, "Let his blood be on us and on our children!" Then he released Barabbas for them. But after he had Jesus flogged, he handed him over to be crucified.[36]

The Death of Christ

In the hands of a Roman executioner, crucifixion was a slow, painful and humiliating death. In fact, though invented by the Persians, the Romans had turned it into something so horrendous and barbaric that it was not only illegal to crucify a Roman citizen, it was virtually unheard of for Roman writers to acknowledge its existence.[37]

Scourging: Many of those who were crucified were "scourged" first. That is, they were tied to a post and flogged with a "cat-of-nine-tails" – a multi-headed whip embedded with bits of bone and sharp metal in its ends – that could strip the flesh off a man's back from his shoulders to his thighs. Some victims died from scourging alone.

Crucifixion: Those who survived the whip were forced to carry their cross to the site of their death. They were stripped of their remaining clothes and either nailed or tied to a cross, which was then dropped into a hole so that it remained upright. The victim was left there – often in a very public setting – to suffer and die.[38]

Those who were scourged generally died quickly. Those who were not whipped first might survive for days, but eventually even they grew too weak to hold themselves upright. They slumped down and struggled to breathe. One of the common ways to speed up death was to break the victim's legs. This left them hanging by their arms and made it almost impossible to take enough weight off of their diaphragm to be able to breathe.

The Final Hours

Jesus was crucified on Friday morning. He was flogged thirty-nine times, a crown of thorns was jammed on his head, he was spit on and mocked and then forced to carry his cross through the streets of Jerusalem towards Golgotha. When he collapsed under its weight, a bystander named Simon was conscripted to help. Around nine o'clock in the morning they arrived at Golgotha, "the place of the skull." Here Jesus was stripped of his clothes, nailed to the cross and propped up between two thieves.

A crowd gathered. While some, such as Mary and the remaining disciples, looked on in horror, others taunted Jesus. He had let them down. A week earlier they had hailed him as king, but when it became clear that he would not lead them where they wanted to go, he had become just another disappointment.

And now Rome had reduced him to little more than a bloody mess.

As Christ grew weaker, and his body began to shut down, the jeering continued.

> Those who passed by hurled insults at him, shaking their heads and saying, "You who are going to destroy the temple and build it in three days, save yourself! Come down from the cross, if you are the Son of God!" In the same way the chief priests, the teachers of the law and the elders mocked him. "He saved others," they said, "but he can't save himself! He's the king of Israel! Let him come down now from the cross, and we will believe in him. He trusts in God. Let God rescue him now if he wants him, for he said, 'I am the Son of God.'"[40]

The Seven Last Words (Sayings) of Christ: Jesus survived for about six hours on the cross. The last three – from noon until around three o'clock in the afternoon – he hung in darkness "for the sun stopped shining."[41] During this time he made seven statements, which are occasionally referred to as the Seven Last Words of Christ.

- **Forgiveness**: In the first final statement, Christ modeled the 'love-your-enemy' response he called others to embrace. Luke wrote, "When they came to the place called 'The Skull,' they crucified him there, along with the criminals, one on his right and one on his left. But Jesus said, 'Father, forgive them, for they don't know what they are doing.'"

- **Salvation**: His second statement involved the two thieves crucified alongside him. When one mocked Jesus – suggesting that if he were really the Messiah he would save himself and them as well – the second thief asked Christ for divine favor.[42] Turning to the first the second one said, "Don't you fear God, since you are under the same sentence of condemnation? And we rightly so, for we are getting what we deserve for what we did, but this man has done nothing wrong." Then he turned to Christ and said, "Jesus, remember me when you come in your kingdom." Jesus replied, "I tell you the truth, today you will be with me in paradise."[43]

- **Relationship**: A bit later Christ made provision for his mother, Mary. She was a widow and he was her oldest son, which, in that culture, meant her wellbeing was not simply his concern, it was also his responsibility. When he saw Mary and John standing close to each other, he looked at her and said, "Woman, behold your son." He then turned to John and said, "Behold your mother."[44]

- **Abandonment**: Not long before his death, Christ quoted the first line of Psalm 22, "Eloi, Eloi, lema sabachthani?" which means, "My God, my God, why have you forsaken me?" Though various interpretations of this statement have been offered, it seems likely that Christ was referencing all of Psalm 22, which is a Psalm of deliverance.[45] It opens with a cry of abandonment and then ends with a celebration of God's provision and care.

- **Distress**: At least once during the six hours Jesus hung on the cross he cried out in thirst. Mark reports that someone from the crowd dipped a sponge in wine mixed with myrrh and held it up to his mouth, but he did not take it. Matthew adds that the wine was also mixed with gall – which would have made it undrinkable – suggesting that what appeared to be an act of kindness was just another form of mockery. [46]

- **Triumph**: Finally, with death just moments away, Jesus cried out "It is finished." It was his announcement that he had completed his assignment. He had introduced the Kingdom of God, he had revealed the Father's love and grace, he had modeled the life we are called to live and he had defeated the powers of darkness. From conception onward he had lived a life of perfect righteousness. And now he had paid our moral debt through his suffering and imminent death. His work was done.

- **Reunion**: With his last words, Christ announced that he was returning to his Father. He was returning to the glory and honor he had left behind when he began to live as one of us. More than that, he was returning to the full fellowship he enjoyed with the Father and the Spirit. Once again, these words come from a Psalm: "Father, into your hands I commit my spirit." [47]

Christ died. Moments after committing his spirit into the care of his Father, Jesus took a final breath and died. It was three o'clock in the afternoon. At that moment the earth shook, rocks split and the veil in the Temple was torn in two. When the centurion standing next to him saw all that had happened, he proclaimed, "Certainly this man was innocent!" He then added, "Truly he was the Son of God."

And Then...

If the story ended with Christ's death you would not be reading about him now. He might have made it into the footnotes of a few ethics textbooks, and it's possible that his name would have been listed alongside other failed, first century Messiahs.[49] But it's more likely that he would have been forgotten about altogether. His followers, including the disciples, would have mourned his death. But they would have eventually moved on. And the church – the global movement which he launched to advance his kingdom – would never have started.

However the story doesn't end here. Less than forty-eight hours after his death, Christ's tomb was empty, and in the days and weeks ahead various groups reported seeing him alive. In fact, people reported meeting with him, touching him, eating with him and listening as he explained how his life, death and resurrection pulled together all of the loose ends of the Hebrew Scriptures. It was from these three things – the empty tomb, his post-resurrection appearances and the perfect way his life and death tied together the Hebrew Scriptures – that faith in Jesus began to spread. And the church – in spite of her many failures – became both the largest, most diverse and longest lasting ideological revolution in the history of the world, and also its premier source of justice and compassion. [50]

But I am getting ahead of myself. We will start with the empty tomb and its implications in the next chapter. First we need to discuss what happened to Christ's body in the hours after his death.

The Hours After Christ's Death

Under normal circumstances the body of a crucified criminal was either left to rot on the cross or tossed into the city dump. [51] Neither happened to Christ. Though most of his followers had fled, two other men stepped forward to care for the body. As soon as Christ died, Joseph of Arimathea, "a highly regarded member of the council, who was himself looking forward to the kingdom of God," asked Pilate for permission to remove Jesus' body from the cross and prepare it for burial. Joseph acted quickly because Sabbath laws forbid any Jew from touching a corpse on the Sabbath, which officially began at sundown on Friday evening, just a few hours after Christ's death.[52]

Mark tells us that Pilate was surprised to hear that Jesus was already dead, so he sent someone to confirm this. John reports these events from a slightly different angle. He notes that just prior to Joseph's request, the Jewish authorities had asked the executioners to break the legs of all three of the men to speed up their death and allow adequate time for the care of their bodies. They did so with the two thieves, but when they came to Jesus they discovered that he was already dead, so they left his legs alone. Nevertheless, "one of the soldiers pierced Jesus' side with a spear, bringing a sudden flow of blood and water."[53]

Christ's Body Was Placed in a Tomb: After being assured that Christ was dead, Pilate gave Joseph permission to take the body. Nicodemus, another Jewish leader who had secretly become a disciple of Christ,[54] stepped in to help. Together the two men took the body to a tomb Joseph owned. There, in the sight of Mary and other women, they hurriedly treated it with about seventy-five pounds of aromatic spices, wrapped it in a linen shroud, rolled a stone in front of the entrance and left.

A Guard was Placed at the Grave: The next morning several members of the Sanhedrin returned to Pilate to express their concern that Christ's body might be stolen.

> The next day, the one after Preparation Day, the chief priests and the Pharisees went to Pilate. "Sir," they said, "we remember that while he was still alive that deceiver said, 'After three days I will rise again.' So give the order for the tomb to be made secure until the third day. Otherwise, his disciples may come and steal the body and tell the people that he has been raised from the dead. This last deception will be worse than the first."
>
> "Take a guard," Pilate answered. "Go, make the tomb as secure as you know how." So they went and made the tomb secure by putting a seal on the stone and posting the guard.[55]

It is not entirely clear whether Pilate was dispatching a Roman military unit or allowing the Jews to post their Temple Guard. Under either scenario the tomb was officially sealed and six to ten men were stationed there to ensure that no one took the body.

This is the way things stood on Saturday morning. Christ lay dead in a guarded tomb and the disciples were in hiding. Everything in their world had pivoted around Jesus and now he was gone. All that remained was disappointment.

ENDNOTES

[1] So much attention is devoted to the final week of Christ's life that some have called the Gospels "Passion Narratives with a long introduction."

[2] See Matthew 20:17-19

[3] In Luke 13:31-33 the Pharisees tell Jesus that he should leave Jerusalem because Herod wants to kill him. Jesus replied: "Go tell that fox, 'I will keep on driving out demons and healing people today and tomorrow, and on the third day I will reach my goal.' In any case, I must press on today and tomorrow and the next day—for surely no prophet can die outside Jerusalem!"

[4] As with several other spots in the Gospels, it is hard to establish an exact sequence of events.

[5] Exodus 12:3-12

[6] See Exodus 12 and 13 for God's instructions about the Passover.

[7] In Matthew 27:46 we read that it was about the ninth hour – which is three o'clock in the afternoon according to first century timekeeping – when Jesus cried out with a loud voice, "Eli, Eli, Lama Sabachthani" and then yielded his Spirit.

[8] People who were crucified generally suffocated when they became too weak to breathe. In an effort to speed up death, executioners would break the victims' legs. This prevented them from pushing up, which prevented them from taking the weight off their diaphragm – which hastened death. In John 19:31-37 we read that when they came by to break Christ's legs – as they did to the two thieves on either side of him – they discovered that He was already dead.

[9] Hebrews 10:4.

[10] Some have suggested that as many as 1,000,000 flooded into Jerusalem for the Passover. Most historians set the number closer to 200,000, noting that this would still be many times the normal population of the city.

[11] Pilate's home was in Caesarea, but he would travel to Jerusalem and stay there during the Passover Festival just in case things got out of hand.

[12] John 11:55ff (The Message)

¹³ Many people had heard about Christ, but, in an era before newspapers, cameras or TV, far fewer knew what he looked like.

¹⁴ Zechariah 9:9f

¹⁵ Two hundred years before Christ was born, after the Maccabees helped liberate the Jews (and Jerusalem) from Syrian oppression, the Jews waved palm branches in celebration and since then, the palm became a national symbol of Judea. When the Romans conquered the area, they minted coins with palm branches on them to celebrate their victory over Judea because the palm was the national symbol of the land.

¹⁶ See John 2:13ff and Mark 11:15-17.

¹⁷ See I Kings 5-8 and 2 Chronicles 1-7 for a description of the Temple.

¹⁸ Following Solomon's death the nation of Israel split in two. Israel – the name retained by the northern 10 tribes – had a series of bad kings, quickly fell into apostasy and was eventually overrun by the Assyrians in 722 BC. These Jews were never heard from again. The southern two tribes – called Judah – lasted longer, but were eventually taken into exile by the Babylonians in 586 BC. After seventy years the Babylonians were defeated by the Persians and the Jews were allowed to return to Jerusalem. Nehemiah led the initial rebuilding effort. The Second Temple was dedicated on March 12, 515 BC. In light of this Jewish history is often divided into three periods: pre-exilic (before the exile), the exile and post-exilic.

¹⁹ Herod the Great was an evil sociopath. He not only ordered the Slaughter of the Innocents, he also had his own wife and sons killed. But he was a brilliant builder. In fact, one historian has suggested that if the Seven Wonders of the World had not already been selected, Herod would have laid claim to about half of them. He built the Temple in an effort to curry favor with the Jews. However, in spite of Herod's conversion to Judaism, marriage into a distinguished Jewish family and efforts to rebuild the temple, never really accepted him.

²⁰ The historian was a Jewish man named Josephus, who became a citizen of Rome. He wrote several books. This reference is taken from, The Jewish War, p. 304.

²¹ The Second Temple would not be finished until almost fifteen years after Christ was crucified. Remarkably, the Romans would destroy all but part of the outside wall in 70 AD after the Jews launched an unsuccessful revolt.

[22] Our God is a temple-dwelling God. First he lived in the midst of the tents with Moses (Ex. 33:13f), then he filled Solomon's Temple with his glory, and finally he "tabernacled" among us through Jesus. When John wrote that "The Word became flesh and dwelt among us," the term translated "dwelt" is the same word for "tabernacle." A tabernacle was "a mobile temple." There are other places where the idea of "Jesus as the Temple" are developed. Two are worth noting. The first comes from the prophet Haggai. There we learn that shortly after the Jews returned from exile and rebuilt the temple - this would be the Second Temple before Herod the Great remodeled it – God promised them that one day the temple would be restored better than ever. Haggai was referring to Jesus when he wrote: "This is what the LORD Almighty says: 'In a little while I will once more shake the heavens and the earth, the sea and the dry land. I will shake all nations, and the desire of all nations will come, and I will fill this house with glory,' says the LORD Almighty." The second reference worth highlighting is found in Rev 21:22, where John reported on his vision of heaven: "And I saw no temple in the city, for its temple is the Lord God the Almighty and the Lamb. And the city has no need of sun or moon to shine upon it, for the glory of God is its light, and its lamp is the Lamb."

[23] Why did the Jewish authorities move against Christ? There were a variety of factors in play: 1) they were uncomfortable with Christ's popularity; 2) he called them "hypocrites, blind guides, white washed tombs, snakes, vipers and sons of the devil:" 3) Pharisees did not like the fact that he had undermined so many of their laws; 4) they were incensed with his claims to be God; and 5) they (especially the Sadducees) feared the instability he introduced.

[24] See also, Mt. 26:3-4.

[25] Luke 22:10-13 suggests that Jesus kept the location of the Passover Meal a secret from everyone except Peter and John. He likely did this so that Judas was unable to tell Roman authorities where he would be. Had they known, they could have arrested Jesus before he had commissioned the Lord's Supper and spent time in prayer.

[26] Israel was instructed to keep the Passover every year, but it had not always done so. In 2 Chronicles 30:1-27 and also later in 35:1-19 we see that there were periods of apostasy where it was not kept.

[27] Mark 14:34-36

[28] Mark 14:41f

29 Mark 14:48

30 The act of tearing your own clothes had precedent in Jewish culture. Reuben and Judah tore their clothes to suggest they were anxious over Joseph's disappearance; Job tore his clothes when told the tragic news about his family and David and his men tore their clothes when they heard about the death of Saul and Jonathan. It was also expected of those who heard blasphemous statements.

31 Mark 14:60ff

32 The Roman historian Philo reports that Pilate was not a man to be messed with. His administration was rife with corruption, strife, injustice, endless brutality and a penchant towards carrying out swift executions without a trial. Within a few years of Christ's death Pilate was removed from office for charges of wanton cruelty and exiled to Gaul.

33 Luke 23:1-2

34 Pilate's wife sent Pilate a note warning him, "not to have anything to do with that innocent man."

35 Some have wondered how those who hailed Christ as king on Sunday could be incited to call for his death on Friday. Several theories have been advanced: 1) some point out that the area in front of Pilate's home was not very large, consequently it could have been a small group chanting for his death; 2) others argue that crowds can be that fickle, and point to sporting events for examples. (People can be considered a hero one moment and a goat the next); 3) a third theory suggests that many were angry with Christ because he had let them down. They wanted a king like David. On Sunday Christ looked like he was going to step into that role. By Friday it was clear that he would not.

36 Matthew 27:22-26

37 Crucifixion was invented by the Persians and employed by the Greeks, but it was made infamous by the Romans. The practice was abolished by Constantine in the fourth century. Roman writers refused to use the word crucifixion because the practice was considered so vile that the word itself would sully their writing. Josephus described crucifixion as "the most wretched of deaths." Cicero was so put off by it that he wrote, "Let the very name of the cross be far away not only from the body of a Roman citizen, but even from his thoughts, eyes, his ears." Of course, the horror associated with crucifixion was even worse for a Jew, for the Hebrew

Scriptures announced that "anyone who hung on a tree was cursed by God" (Josephus, Jewish War 5:11.1 (450), 7:6.4); Cicero, Pro Rairio 5; Deut. 21:23). It is worth quoting C.S. Lewis who noted that "crucifixion did not become common in art, nor the cross a piece of jewelry until all who had witnessed it died off."

[38] It is hard to overstate the physical and emotional trauma that accompanied crucifixion. Victims were generally stripped naked, spikes were pounded through the nerve centers in their hands and feet, and they were left to suffer, often at a busy intersection or just outside the city gate.

[39] It was commonly believed that no one could survive forty lashes. Jesus received thirty-nine.

[40] Matthew 27:39-43

[41] Luke 23:44

[42] Matthew reports that both of the criminals being crucified next to Christ mocked him. Luke's report suggests that at some point one of the two softened.

[43] There was no punctuation in the original Greek. This has led to two different interpretations of this passage. Protestants understand Christ's statement to read, "Today you will be with me in Paradise. Roman Catholic translations render it, "I tell you today, you will (eventually) be with me in Paradise." This second translation allows for time to be spent in Purgatory, a doctrine Protestants do not endorse.

[44] John 19:26-27

[45] Before the Bible was divided into chapters (the 13th century) and verses (the 16th century) it was common for people to reference a passage, especially a Psalm, by reciting the first line.

[46] John's account (Jn 19:28-30) contains the suggestion that Jesus asked for something to drink in order to fulfill a prophecy about the Messiah. See Psalm 22:15 and 69:21.

[47] Ps. 31:5 and Luke 23:46

[48] The guard's statement is remarkable for several reasons: 1) as a guard he among all others would be expected to declare that Caesar was 'the Son of God;' 2) he would be inclined to say that someone who was victorious in battle or had great power over others was the "Son of God," not a poor,

humiliated, crucified Jew. But standing next to Christ's lifeless body he declared, "Surely this man was the Son of God." (Mark 15:39)

[49] The decades around the time of Christ saw dozens of would-be Messiahs. In virtually every case the man was killed and the movement collapsed.

[50] The church has not always lived up to her call – and has even had periods of significant darkness – but Christians working together to honor God and serve others have not only built schools, hospitals and orphanages but have also helped establish rule of law, fought slavery and advanced other humanitarian causes.

[51] Following a slave revolt in 71 BC Rome crucified 6,000 men. They spaced the crosses along 100 miles of the Appian Way – a road leading into Rome – and let the bodies rot on the cross as a warning to those who were considering challenging Rome's power.

[52] The Jewish Sabbath begins with sundown on Friday and continues until sundown on Saturday.

[53] In addition to confirming that Jesus was dead, John notes (Jn 19:33ff) that these two things happened – i.e., Christ's legs were left unbroken but his side was pierced – in order that the scripture would be fulfilled. "Not one of his bones will be broken," and, as another scripture says, "They will look on the one they have pierced."

[54] Nicodemus' late night visit with Christ is recorded in John 3:1-21.

[55] Matthew 27:62

CHAPTER 5
King of Kings - From Death to Glory

If Christ is risen, nothing else matters. If Christ is not risen, nothing else matters.
Jaroslav Pelikan

On the third day he rose again. He ascended into Heaven and sits at the right hand of God the Father Almighty.
The Apostles' Creed

Despite our efforts to keep him out, God intrudes. The life of Jesus is bracketed by two impossibilities: a virgin's womb and an empty tomb. Jesus entered our world through a door marked, "No Entrance" and he left through a door marked "No Exit."
Peter Larson

When we left Jesus, his lifeless body was lying cold and still inside a guarded tomb.

His last week had started with great promise. He had paraded into Jerusalem as a popular hero and would-be king. Hopes were high, flags were waving and the people were shouting "Hosanna." But everything unraveled pretty quickly after that. On Wednesday evening he was betrayed. Very early on Friday morning he was arrested, and by 9 a.m. of that day Roman executioners were driving spikes through his hands and feet.

It was over soon after that. The people jeered, the afternoon sky turned dark and Jesus suffered and died as a cursed and despised criminal.

The big question is, what happened next? Exactly what transpired in the early hours of Sunday morning? There appear to be two options. Either Jesus defeated death and rose from the grave, confirming his claims to be the Son of God and Savior of the World, or something else happened that led a lot of people to think he did. And those who were misled – whether it was through a deliberate hoax or an unwitting mix-up – ended up misleading others, who in turn misled others, until this mistaken belief was on its way around the world.

Both options are shocking. On the one hand we have God Almighty, King of Kings and Lord of Lords, showing up as a first-century Jewish carpenter, and on the other we have several billion people basing their life on a sham. For a number of reasons – both historical and personal – I believe the first choice is the right one, and in the course of this study I want to explain why. But before we turn there I want to set the resurrection in context. In one sense it stands on its own as the defining event that separates Jesus from every other moral and religious leader – he conquered death and they did not. But in another, it can only be appreciated if it's seen as the culmination and confirmation of a much bigger story. I want to be sure you see Christ's crucifixion and resurrection as the axis around which everything rotates.

The Claim

The crux of what I've been arguing over the last 100 pages can be summarized in six points.

One: The Bible is the Story of our Rescue. The Bible is not a random collection of morality lessons and inspirational anecdotes. It is the story of God's efforts to rescue us and restore his kingdom. In all of this, Jesus is the star. The Old Testament points ahead to his arrival. The Gospels point ahead to the final week of his life, and the rest of the New Testament points back to his death and resurrection.[1]

Two: Jesus is God. Jesus is not just the Jewish Messiah, nor is he almost God, God-like, God-lite, god with a small "g," or the Vice President of Heaven. He is fully God and equal to the Father. There never has been, nor will there ever be, anyone like him.

Three: Jesus was born to die. Jesus existed as God from the very beginning. At the appointed time he "took on flesh," adding humanity to deity and showing up in the backwaters of the Roman Empire to rescue us. He did this out of love and in compliance with his Father's plan. During his time on earth Jesus passed the test that Adam failed, revealed God's true nature, modeled how to live, fulfilled the Law and inaugurated the kingdom. But his principal task was to suffer the death we deserve. A careful review of the biblical text makes several things clear:

- **Christ's death was planned.** The crucifixion was not an accident. It was foretold in Genesis 3, predicted by the prophets and described in detail hundreds of years before it happened.[2] Jesus did not lose his life because of some political miscalculations. He willingly laid it down as part of a plan. Christ was born to die. In fact, he paraded into Jerusalem with the cross in mind.

- **Christ's death was necessary.** God's holiness and love combined to make the cross necessary. The first made it impossible for him to ignore our sin. The second made it impossible for him to walk away. Only by dying in our place could God satisfy the demands of both justice and love. [3]

- **Christ's death was horrible.** Few deaths are as horrific as crucifixion[4], but the physical pain Jesus endured was insignificant compared to the spiritual agony. There is no calculus that allows us to understand how much Christ suffered on our behalf.[5]

- **Christ's death was transformational.** Christ's death changed everything. It did away with the need for both sacrifices and the Temple.[6] It brought clear focus on the covenant of grace. It gave us direct and immediate access to the Father. The life and death of Jesus of Nazareth erased our debt, secured our justification and inaugurated the Kingdom of God on earth.

Four: Jesus rose from the dead. Right alongside Christ's amazing death was his supernatural resurrection. About forty hours after his body was placed in the tomb, Jesus crossed back over the dark divide and emerged as the "first born of the dead."[7]

- This was not a simple *resuscitation*, such as Lazarus had already undergone. Lazarus' life was restored, but he would later die a second time. Jesus was raised immortal and imperishable. He had returned with a body that would last forever.

- This was not simply a *spiritual resurrection* – where his soul lived on but his body remained in the grave. Christ was neither a ghost nor an apparition. He was flesh and blood. He had risen in the "self-same"[8] body in which he had died.

- Finally, his resurrection was not a metaphor. Christ was not "living on in people's hearts," present each time "the sun rises" or "alive again in every child's laughter." When the apostles spoke about Christ's resurrection they were making an historical claim not a religious one. This was not the stuff of folklore, myth or legend. It was history. Jesus had really lived, really died and really returned from the dead.[9]

For Paul, the resurrection changed everything. It explained Christ's miracles, validated his life and supported his claims. It was the linchpin. Had Jesus remained in the grave there would be no reason to follow him or believe any of his other claims – and there certainly would not be any reason to worship him. In fact, according to Paul, if Christ did not rise from the dead then Christianity was a bad joke. But since he did rise from the dead there was every reason to trust his other claims as well.

Five: The Story does not end with the resurrection. Christ's life not only started before Christmas, it continued after Easter. In the days after he rose from the dead Jesus did five significant things:

- **He explained the story**. The disciples had never really understood who Jesus was or what he was doing. In fact, even when they seemed to get it – such as Peter's Confession – it later became clear that they had not. This changed during the forty days Christ spent on earth between his resurrection and ascension. During this time he "began with Moses and all the prophets and explained to them what was said in all the Scriptures concerning himself."[10] They finally understood who he was and what his death had accomplished.

- **He commissioned the church.** At the end of the forty days Christ gathered his disciples on a mountain in Galilee and gave them a final charge, instructing them to spread his kingdom by proclaiming the Good News and engaging in good works. The last words of Matthew's Gospel record this "Great Commission." They read:

> Then Jesus came to them and said, 'All authority in heaven and on earth has been given to me. Therefore go and make

disciples of all nations, baptizing them in the name of the
Father and of the Son and of the Holy Spirit, and teaching
them to obey everything I have commanded you. And surely I
am with you always, to the very end of the age.'

- **He ascended into heaven.** Shortly after charging his followers to
carry on his work, Christ slowly rose up through the sky and into
heaven itself. Luke describes the Ascension in two places. At the end
of his Gospel we read, "When he had led them out to the vicinity
of Bethany, he lifted up his hands and blessed them. While he was
blessing them, he left them and was taken up into heaven. Then they
worshiped him and returned to Jerusalem with great joy." He also
opens the Book of Acts by retelling the event, stating that Jesus was,
"...taken up before their very eyes, and a cloud hid him from their
sight."[11] The word used here for "cloud" is the same term used in
other places to describe the glory that accompanies the presence of
God.

- **He was crowned King of Kings:** The fourth thing Jesus did was full
of royal symbolism: he sat down in the place of highest honor - the
right hand of his Father. Christ did not simply levitate into the sky – he
was received into heaven as King of Kings.[12] Paul used the words of
a first-century hymn to describe this event. It begins by noting that
Christ humbled himself by becoming man and dying on a cross,
before proclaiming that the Father consequently "exalted him to the
highest place, and gave him the name that is above every name, that
at the name of Jesus every knee should bow, in heaven and on earth
and under the earth, and every tongue acknowledge that Jesus Christ
is Lord, to the glory of God the Father." As a result of his service
on earth, God the Father exalted Jesus to the highest place in the
universe.[13] No one has ever descended lower or been exalted higher
than Jesus.

- **He sent the Holy Spirit:** One of the very first things Christ did as King
was to send the Holy Spirit to indwell and empower his followers.
In Acts 2 we read that the Spirit of God "fell upon" those gathered
in the Upper Room, and that under this supernatural empowerment
they preached the Gospel in other languages and many came to faith.

This indwelling changed everything. From this point on the disciples moved forward with a courage and zeal they had not previously shown.[14]

Six: The Story Continues. The Book of Acts records what happened after Pentecost. In fact, it documents the next thirty years, during which time the church expanded beyond Jerusalem and Judea and moved into Rome. During the next several hundred years those who affirmed the deity of Christ grew in number and influence until Christianity became the dominant view in Europe. Today the church is the largest, oldest, most influential and most ethnically- and geographically-diverse movement in the world.[15]

And the story does not end here. According to the Bible, four events remain:

- Christ will return: At the appointed hour Jesus will return to earth, only this time he will not arrive as a helpless infant but as a conquering King. When he does, everything will be brought under his rule and reign.

- The dead will rise. At the time Christ returns, the souls of everyone who has ever lived will be reunited with their resurrected bodies. With these new bodies we will be prepared for eternity.[16]

- Christ will judge each of us. Every person will stand accountable for the life they have lived. Those who have repented of their sin and been redeemed by Christ will have their works reviewed at the Judgment Seat of Christ. Fire will burn away the "wood, hay and stubble" of activities of no value, leaving some with "gold, silver and precious stones" and others with a sense of regret for selfish choices and lost opportunity. However, the overwhelming emotion for all believers will be one of joy at the chance to enter into the immediate presence of Christ. In contrast, those who stand on their own – without Christ as Savior – will have their life reviewed at the Great White Throne Judgment, fall short of his glory and be removed to the Abyss.[17]

- Christ will restore a New Heaven and New Earth. In the end, God's initial plans will finally and fully be realized. The tragic delay caused by sin will be no more. A new heaven and a new earth will be revealed. Death – which had previously been defeated – will be destroyed, Christ will be exalted and the children of God will enjoy life with God in its fullest.

Future events raise lots of questions. We will take up a few of them in our final chapter. But right now we return to the critical question: Is this story true? Is Jesus God? Did he rise from the dead?

It All Comes Down to the Resurrection

In the end, it all comes down to the resurrection. There are a host of other arguments that could be made in support of the Christian faith - we could review the cosmological, ontological and teleological arguments for the existence of God, study the archeological and bibliographic support for the New Testament, ponder the brilliance of Christ's ethics, calculate the odds of anyone accidentally fulfilling the Messianic prophecies he did, or pour over the stories of the hundreds of millions of people who claim Jesus changed their lives. There is real value in all of these. But in the end, it all turns on the resurrection. Did Jesus rise from the dead or not?

Christ did not claim to be a great teacher who should be listened to, he claimed to be to the Creator of the universe who should be worshipped. Part of that claim included the promise to defeat death. Either he defeated death or he didn't. If he did, we have every reason to believe all of his other claims – i.e., he is Lord, God and King. If he did not, then all bets are off – he's an interesting figure but little more. In fact, if Jesus didn't rise from the dead then the only material difference between him and all of the other would-be Messiahs is that he not only failed to liberate the Jews, he also got caught in a wild and malicious lie. After all, he claimed to be God and they did not.

As the early church announced, Jesus is either God or a bad man, and everything turns on the resurrection.

So, did Christ rise or didn't he?

Here is what virtually everyone agrees on, including honest skeptics.[18]

- Christ died around three o'clock on Friday afternoon.
- In the few hours between his last breath and sunset – when Sabbath laws would prevent law-abiding Jews from touching a corpse – his body was taken off the cross, treated with seventy-five to eighty pounds of spices, wrapped in a linen sheet and placed in a garden tomb.
- The next morning Pilate agreed to the Jewish leaders' request to have a military unit guard the tomb. They did this to ensure that no one stole the body.
- Nevertheless, when Mary, Mary Magdalene and Salome arrived at the tomb on Sunday morning they discovered that the stone sealing its entrance had been rolled away and the body was gone. They also reported that Jesus appeared to them, that he was alive and well, and that he had instructed them to go tell others.
- Over the next few weeks hundreds of other people reported seeing, talking to and touching Jesus.
- The belief that Christ had risen from the grave launched the Christian faith.

The critical question is: what happened to the body – where did it go? Millions of people have wrestled with this question. Thousands have devoted years of their lives to studying it. A number of different theories have been advanced; in the end they break into six camps.[19]

Option One: Jesus did not die on the cross

Some people contend that Jesus did not die on the cross – he simply fainted from a loss of blood and later revived in the cool of the tomb. This is known as the Swoon Theory.

In order to embrace this option we must believe that:

- Though Jesus was exhausted, traumatized and hemorrhaging immense amounts of blood, he merely lost consciousness on the cross. Indeed, he remained alive even after the Roman executioner thrust a spear into his side.

- Neither the professional executioner nor those treating his body ever noticed that he was still alive.

- He not only survived being mummified and then sealed in a tomb without food, water or air for around forty hours, he somehow got better.

- After he regained consciousness he was able to wriggle out of his tightly wrapped shroud, push back the massive stone, overpower the Roman soldiers and walk several miles on pierced feet.

- Instead of reaching the obvious conclusion – i.e., Jesus had somehow survived a botched crucifixion – those who saw him were tricked into believing that he had entered a glorious new dimension of life.

- After being hailed the risen Son of God he slipped away to live the rest of his life in obscurity.

Beyond the obvious weaknesses of this theory, several more emerge with additional study.

- We need to remember that Jesus was not simply crucified; he was first beaten and flogged. The latter was so brutal that many died from it alone. In fact, it was widely held that no one could survive forty lashes – Jesus received thirty-nine. Without immediate medical care he likely would have died from the flogging and infection that followed, even if he had not been crucified.[22]

- Roman executioners who failed to kill their prisoner were killed for their incompetence. They were not known to make mistakes.

- Pilate did not initially accept Joseph of Arimathea's claim that Jesus was dead; instead he asked the guards confirm it. When the executioners checked on Christ they determined that he had already died and consequently did not bother to break his legs as was the custom. Nevertheless, one of them rammed a spear into his side, producing a flow of 'blood and water.' Modern medical experts suggest that these symptoms point in one of two directions: either the trauma Christ experienced caused fluid to build up in the pericardial sac surrounding his heart, or the blood inside the heart itself had started to separate into plasma and red blood cells. Either situation was a clear indication of death.[23]

There are other problems with this theory – it requires us to believe that the world's greatest ethical system was established by a con man, and suggests that Christ fulfilled all of the Messianic prophecies by chance. But these are enough to doom it.[24]

Option Two: It was a group hallucination

The second theory goes something like this: the disciples were so disappointed when Jesus died that they refused to accept it. Instead they collectively willed themselves into imagining that he rose from the dead. As theories go, this one is easy to suggest but hard to defend. To start with, it does nothing to explain the empty tomb or the fulfilled prophecy. Additionally, it violates almost everything we know about hallucinations.

- Hallucinations are typically associated with people who are either neurotic or actually psychotic, but those who claim to have seen Jesus not only include "the distressed women but also the hot-tempered John, the aggressive Peter, an ordered public servant like Matthew, a brilliant intellectual like Paul and a stubborn skeptic like Thomas."[25]

- Hallucinations usually occur in favorable settings and at times when a person is wrapped in sentimental feelings. But hardly any of the reported appearances fit those circumstances. They were not in places where Jesus had spent time with his followers; instead they occurred in places filled with stress and confusion.

- Hallucinations are individual experiences tied to a person's own subconscious. Yet the New Testament reports that Jesus not only appeared to individuals, he also appeared to groups of two, three, seven and at one point over five hundred. In each case, everyone reported seeing the same thing. This is not how hallucinations work. It may be that many people hallucinate at the same time - Woodstock comes to mind – but they do not share the same hallucination.

Some moderns wrongly imagine that the citizens of the first century were unsophisticated naïfs who readily – and easily – embraced the resurrection. This is not true. The followers of Jesus were initially skeptical of Christ's appearances. The women who had gone to the tomb had done so to embalm Jesus, not embrace him. When the women told the disciples that he was alive the disciples did not believe them.[26] Thomas went so far as to say, "Unless I see the nail marks in his hands and put my finger where the nails were, and put my hand into his side, I will not believe."[27] And Mark reports that Jesus later "rebuked them for their unbelief and hardness of heart, because they had not believed those who saw him after he had risen."[28]

Paul's vision of Christ came after the excitement of seeing Jesus had died down. And far from wanting to believe the earlier reports, Paul was on his way to arrest those who were spreading them. He was convinced that Christ's resurrection was a deadly lie. His vision of the risen Christ was not the result of wishful thinking. It was about the worst news he could imagine. He only believed it because the evidence persuaded him that it was true.

Option Three: The Women Went to the Wrong Tomb

In 1907 a British scholar named Kirsopp Lake advanced a new idea. He claimed the three women going to care for Christ's body had gone to the wrong tomb. Overwhelmed with grief and unable to see clearly in the dim light of the early morning, they had become lost. Spotting a cemetery worker they asked for directions. The caretaker responded, "You are looking for Jesus of Nazareth. He is not here." He then pointed to the correct tomb, but the women misunderstood him, decided that he was actually an angel and that he had been sent to announce that Christ had risen from the dead. This theory gets points for creativity, but not many for viability. Three factors overwhelm it.

First, Mark 15 reports that two of the three women had been present for Jesus' burial just thirty-six hours earlier. They "saw where he was laid." The word translated "saw" represents a person who looks on "with interest and for a purpose, usually indicating a careful observation of details." Having recently returned from Israel I can add that the Old City of Jerusalem is small and the first-century burial sites are quite close. A fifteen minute walk (at most) takes you to them. It's hard to imagine anyone getting lost in an area they would know so well, or anyone accepting the resurrection without checking out the tomb themselves.

Second, Lake bases his theory on some creative editing of Mark 16, which reports that after entering the tomb:

> The women saw a young man dressed in a white robe sitting on the right side, and they were alarmed. "Don't be alarmed," he said. "You are looking for Jesus the Nazarene, who was crucified. He has risen! He is not here. See the place where they laid him. But go, tell his disciples and Peter, 'He is going ahead of you into Galilee. There you will see him, just as he told you.'"

Lake leaves most of the text out – starting with the angel's announcement that Jesus was risen.

Finally, in order for the Wrong Tomb theory to be true, it's not just the women who need to get it wrong, everyone else must as well. When Peter and John heard that Jesus had risen from the dead they ran to the tomb to see for themselves. The sun would have been up by then. Are we to suppose that they also went to the wrong tomb? One of the Marys later returned to the tomb. Did she get it wrong a second time? What about the Roman guards – were they posted at the wrong tomb? What about Joseph? He owned the tomb. Are we to imagine that he never went to the right tomb and discovered the body? For that matter, what about the Jewish and Roman authorities? They were motivated to discredit Christianity. Without the resurrection this new sect would collapse. They possessed the means, motive and opportunity to find the body and put an end to everything. Are we to suppose that none of them ever went to the tomb to check things out for themselves?

It's worth adding that even if everyone went to the wrong tomb, this theory does nothing to explain the post-resurrection appearances of Christ, his fulfillment of Messianic prophecies or the transformation of the disciples.

Option Four: Jesus Had a Secret Look-a-Like

The fourth theory is based on the idea that someone who looked exactly like Jesus had been waiting in the shadows to step in at the appropriate moment. This person (a twin?) either died in Jesus' place as the ultimate stunt double, or he presented himself as Christ after Jesus had been crucified.

This theory has never gained much traction for a handful of reasons. First, there is absolutely no evidence for it. Second, anyone wishing to present themselves as the risen Christ needed to dispose of the real Christ's body first. This immediately brings us back to the Roman guards standing watch at a sealed tomb. How were they overcome? Third, it is hard to believe that someone other than Christ could persuade those who had been close to Christ – i.e., the disciples, Mary, etc. – that they were Jesus. He had only been away for a few days. If your best friend went away for a three-day weekend and then someone else tried to take their place, do you think they impersonator could trick you? Fourth, Thomas only believed after he put his hands in the holes in Christ's hands and feet. Did the imitation Christ inflict these wounds on himself? The list goes on – where did the substitute go after forty days? How were Christ's miracles performed? Why was any of this done? As I noted, this theory has been panned by most everyone.

Option Five: Someone Stole the Body

From the very earliest days some have argued that Christ's body was stolen. Those in this camp accept that he died, was buried in Joseph's tomb and that the body disappeared before Sunday morning. But they do not believe that he rose from the dead. Instead, they contend that one of four groups stole the body: the Roman authorities, the Jewish leaders, a group of grave robbers or the disciples. Let's consider each group separately.

The Roman Authorities: The idea that Roman leaders had Christ's body removed is a nonstarter for one main reason – there is no motive. The Empire depended upon stability. This is why they crucified Christ and posted a guard at his tomb. Additionally, they had enough problems in Judea without word leaking out that their executioners were inept and their legionnaires couldn't guard a grave site. Pilate had literally and symbolically washed his hands of Jesus. He wanted everything about Christ to go away. Stirring things up was not a part of their plan. The Romans may have had the means and the opportunity to steal Christ's body, but they lacked anything approaching a motive.

The Jewish Leaders: This theory also dies before it starts. And once again it dies for lack of motive. An empty tomb was the Jewish leaders' worst fear. Christ had promised that he would rise on the third day. His integrity and identity now depended upon it. The members of the Sanhedrin only needed to ensure that the body was still in the grave on the fourth day. This is why they had asked Pilate to post a guard at the tomb.

After the body went missing the Jewish leaders had those who spoke about it arrested, imprisoned, threatened and flogged. All of this would have been unnecessary if they had the body. In fact, they could have shut the whole movement down by putting Christ's body in a cart and wheeling it into the center of Jerusalem.

If the Jewish leaders had stolen the body – or had any idea where it was – they could have put a quick end to their problems. They did not. As the Scottish theologian Andrew Fairbairn has said, "The silence of the Jews is as significant as the speech of the Christians."[31]

Grave Robbers: Very few people rob graves, and those who do would not steal the body, they would steal the gold, jewelry and other valuables buried with it. In the off chance that someone was unbalanced enough to steal a body, it's unlikely they would decide to rob the one tomb that is being guarded by Roman soldiers. It's equally unlikely that they would take time during the theft to unwrap the body from its burial shroud, neatly refold the sheet and then leave it in the tomb.[32]

The disciples: The idea that the disciples stole the body is one of the earliest explanations put forward. In fact, it's found in Matthew 28, where we read:

> While the women were on their way, some of the guards went into the city and reported to the chief priests everything that had happened. When the chief priests had met with the elders and devised a plan, they gave the soldiers a large sum of money, telling them, "You are to say, 'His disciples came during the night and stole him away while we were asleep.' If this report gets to the governor, we will satisfy him and keep you out of trouble." So the soldiers took the money and did as they were instructed. And this story has been widely circulated among the Jews to this very day.

Were the disciples capable of stealing the body? It seems unlikely for a handful of reasons. First, the task required a level of leadership, planning and courage they had failed to display when Christ was alive. It seems doubtful they could pull off something this bold in his absence.

Second, a review of the details suggests that the disciples not only lacked the means, they also lacked a motive. Some skeptics have mistakenly looked at the wealth of the church today and assumed that the disciples were selfishly motivated to keep the movement together – that there were assets to protect, money to be made and power to be gained by persuading people that Jesus was still alive. This is not true. Believing that the disciples stole the body not only requires us to assume that they were willing to lie to everyone, it also ignores the perils they faced in promoting the idea that Christ did rise. From an earthly perspective, the only thing the disciples got out of claiming that Christ rose from the dead was a hard life and an early death.

The final reason to dismiss this theory is the steadfast convictions of the disciples over the next thirty years. During this time they were hated, scorned, excommunicated, beaten, imprisoned and tortured. Ten of them were martyred. And yet, at no point did any of them waiver from their claim: the tomb was empty because Jesus was God. Few people will die for the truth. Are we to believe that these men died for a lie?

The late Charles Colson, who served as chief counsel to President Nixon before being sent to prison for his role in the Watergate scandal, dismissed this idea in light of his own experiences. He writes:

> In my Watergate experience I saw the inability of men – powerful, highly motivated professionals – to hold together a conspiracy based on a lie... Yet Christ's followers maintained to their grim deaths by execution that they had in fact seen Jesus Christ raised from the dead. There was no conspiracy. Men do not give up comfort – and certainly not their lives – for what they know to be a lie.[34]

Some are willing to die for something they believe to be true (and countless have done so). But nobody is prepared to die for something they know to be false.

It is possible that the disciples were mistaken about Christ's resurrection. But the transformation of their lives and the unwavering nature of their testimony make it clear that they believed Christ rose from the dead.[35] They did not steal the body.

Option Six: Christ Rose From The Dead

The final explanation for the empty tomb is the one found in the Bible itself. It is the belief that Jesus is who he claimed to be – the Savior of the World and Son of God – and that he did what he promised he would do – defeat death and rise again.

Here are eight of the many reasons to hold to this view.

One: The resurrection pulls everything together. It's worth taking three steps back and reviewing the big picture. The Bible is a collection of sixty-six books written over sixteen hundred years by forty different authors in three languages and on three continents – and the whole thing pivots around the crucifixion and resurrection of Jesus Christ. Everything written before these two events is pointing ahead to them; everything written later is pointing back. Those who discount the resurrection are not harmlessly ignoring a trifling matter, they are yanking on the thread that unravels the entire tapestry. If you throw out the resurrection, the only thing you are left with is questions: If Jesus wasn't the Son of God then who was he? Where did he get such profound wisdom? How did he pull off his miracles? How did he turn twelve also-rans into a force that humbled the Roman Empire? How could he fulfill so many prophecies? Who started the story that he rose from the dead? How did the tomb end up empty?

Two: The initial eye-witnesses were women. Women were not allowed to testify in first-century Jewish or Roman courts because they were not believed to be trustworthy witnesses. It follows that if someone had set out to fabricate the resurrection they would not have had women be the first to view the risen Christ, especially a woman with Mary Magdalene's questionable past. They would have had a highly influential male leader instead.[37]

Three: The Gospel accounts sound authentic. The Gospel reports of Christ's resurrection read exactly like what they claim to be – first and second hand accounts of a real event. For instance, Mark reports that when the women entered the tomb, "they saw a young man dressed in a white robe sitting on the right side." Luke reports that after they discovered the tomb was empty, "two men in clothes that gleamed like lightning stood beside them." Matthew's account mentions "an angel of the Lord" who was at the tomb." Which is it? Were they angels or men? Were there one or two?

Some have pointed to these verses[38] as a contradiction in the Bible.[39] Those who are used to reading multiple accounts of a single event see these reports as authentic accounts. In fact, far from being troubled with the initial discrepancies, they are leery of multiple accounts of the same story that are too perfect. To put it simply – whenever everyone is saying exactly the same thing, someone is copying off of someone else, or they all agreed beforehand on what they were going to write. These accounts sound like authentic reports from firsthand and second hand witnesses.

Four: Something happened to change the date of worship. The first church gatherings were comprised exclusively of Jews or Jewish proselytes. Their understanding of the fourth commandment – to say nothing of their practice over thousands of years – led them to worship God on Saturday. Something major had to happen to cause them to move their sacred day of rest and worship.

Five: Something happened to change the object of worship. It's not just that the Jews moved their Sabbath from Saturday to Sunday, they extended their worship to include Jesus as well. This is extraordinary. At the very top of the list of Jewish affirmation is the understanding that there is only one God. And yet, even before anyone had articulated the Triune nature of God, the Jews began worshipping the Son of God alongside the Father God.

Six: Jesus had predicted his resurrection. Christ had frequently alluded to his death. This is unremarkable in itself; after all, everyone is going to die, so predicting your own death is an exercise in stating the obvious. However, Christ went beyond this. He never spoke about his death without also claiming that he would rise again. He even pinpointed how long he would be dead before he would rise.[40]

Seven: The changed lives of the disciples. Most legends start generations after the death of the first hand witnesses. The Christian faith did not. In fact, it started right after Pentecost and it was started by those closest to the events. As was noted above, the disciples morphed from timid and clueless followers to bold and fearless witnesses. They did this in response to their belief that Jesus had risen.[41]

Eight: Christ was the most amazing person to ever live. Finally, it's worth reminding ourselves that the resurrection was not a remarkable ending to an otherwise un-remarkable life; it was the capstone miracle of the most amazing life ever. As we noted in the first chapter, Jesus stands above all others. He lived a sinless life. He taught with authority, healed the sick, multiplied food, walked on water, quieted storms and raised the dead. Claiming that Christ conquered death is not like claiming that you or I did. That would be amazing. Jesus is the most interesting and important person who has ever lived. He did the most amazing things that have ever been done. He claimed to be God, predicted his death and promised to rise again on the third day. Given all the facts, it would have been more remarkable if Jesus hadn't defeated death.

So Now What?

There is more that could be said, but I believe it's time to call the question. You have a decision to make. Sherlock Holmes said, "When you have eliminated the impossible, whatever remains, however improbable, must be the truth." C.S. Lewis brought that logic to the person of Christ, writing:

> We are faced, then, with a frightening alternative. The man we are talking about was and is just what he said or else insane or something worse. Now, it seems to me obvious that he was neither insane nor a fiend; and consequently, however strange or terrifying or unlikely it may seem, I have to accept the view that he was and is God.

Are you persuaded? I hope so. I believe that Christ's claims, warnings and promises are all true, and that placing your faith in him is the best decision you could ever make. Through Christ, God will forgive you and welcome you into his family as an adopted son or daughter. You will gain eternal life, be filled with God's Spirit and become part of the expanding Kingdom of God.[42]

One of the reasons these studies were written was to persuade you to do just that. Taking a next step does not require a blind leap of faith. As I hope is clear by now, there are good reasons for you to believe that Jesus is God.

This does, however, require you to take action – to go beyond giving a simple head-nod to God or affirming that Christ is God. Becoming a Christ-follower involves repenting of your sins and placing your hope in Christ. It engages both your mind and your heart. God is not forcing your hand. There is not enough evidence to persuade those who chose not to believe. But there is an open invitation for those who do. If you would like to take a next step, I invite you to pray the following prayer.

> Lord Jesus Christ, I am sorry for the things I have done wrong in my life. I am sorry for my selfishness, greed, pride, anger and many other sins. Please forgive me. Thank you for dying on the cross so that I could be forgiven. I now turn from everything I know that is wrong. Spirit of God, thank you for coming to live in me now. Please guide and direct my path. Help me to become more like you. Thank you. Amen

ENDNOTES

[1] Christ is assumed in Genesis 1, introduced in Genesis 3 and alluded to in Genesis 12. Though he never walks on center stage in the Old Testament, he is never far off it either. The Law and sacrificial systems were established to help people see their need for him, and the prophets kept reminding people that he was coming. Granted, the plan took much longer to unfold than anyone seemed to expect, but the Old Testament laid the foundation for him to arrive, and then the Gospels devote the bulk of their attention to the final week of Christ's life. Finally, the rest of the New Testament documents point back to the crucifixion and resurrection. The Bible reveals God's unfolding plan to restore his work, starting with the restoration of those he made in his image.

[2] One of the ways to show that Christ's death was planned is to show that it was predicted. One thousand years before he was born the Psalmist described the Messiah's death by writing, "they pierced my hands and my feet." (Note: This was written hundreds of years before crucifixion was even invented.) Several hundred years later – but still 700 years before Christ was born – Isaiah added additional details, such as the fact that he would be

killed alongside the wicked (thieves) yet buried with the rich (he was buried in Joseph of Arimathea's tomb). See also: Mark 8:31; 9:31; 10:33-34 and Luke 13:32f.

[3] Some have argued that a benevolent God could simply accept us as we are. However, that argument minimizes both the magnitude of God's holiness and the seriousness of our sin. Our debt must be atoned for. God's plan satisfies justice while demonstrating love. Indeed, it demonstrates the greatest love of all, that of one who would lay down his life for another.

[4] The Romans had some interest in justice, but they also had a large interest in deterrence. They wanted crucifixion to be so horrible and humiliating that it would deter people from acting out against the state.

[5] Some believe that Christ's final cry – "My God, My God, why have you forsaken me?" (Ps. 22) – indicates that the Father turned his back on the Son; that is, that the perfect fellowship which had existed from eternity past between the Father, Son and Holy Spirit was broken apart, at least for a moment, when Christ became sin. Others hold that what happened fell just short of that. The spiritual and emotional anguish experienced by Christ on the cross when he bore my sin (and yours) is beyond our comprehension. But the Father was in the Son acted together on our behalf.

[6] At the time of Christ's death the veil that separated the Holy of Holies from the rest of the Temple was ripped from the top to the bottom – i.e., it was ripped by God. The theological significance of this act was profound. It meant that through Christ's sacrificial death his followers were now able to approach God directly, as long as they did so in Christ's name. Christians no longer needed a Temple, nor did they need to offer a sacrifice or go through an earthly priest, they (we) could now approach God the Father anywhere and anytime via Jesus Christ, our High Priest.

[7] Most first-century Jews believed the same thing that many people currently believe, that at the time of our death some aspect of our soul lives on. Therefore, they would not have been shocked to hear that Christ was spiritually alive. But that is not what happened. Christ's body had come back to life. He was not a ghost or some kind of spirit, he was physically alive. The disciples clung to his feet (Mt. 28:9), Thomas touched him (Jn 20:24-29), Mary saw and spoke to him (Jn 20:14-17), he ate food in front of them (Lk 24:36-43). He went out of his way to prove that he had risen physically from the dead.

[8] "Self-same" is a term used by the early Christians to describe Christ's resurrection body. In some ways it was the same body that had died. In other ways it was different – i.e., it was immortal and Christ apparently

looked slightly different than he had before. (Some have speculated that he was a bit younger, and that when we are resurrected we will all be 29 – the perfect age!). In any event, when the New Testament writers refer to Christ's resurrection body they are clear that it was real flesh and blood.

[9] J.B. Phillips famously suggested that the early Christians "gossiped the Gospel" throughout the Roman Empire. To the extent that this was true, they gossiped the resurrection. The idea that Christ had come back from the dead was one of the best known aspects of the Christian faith. Confirming this are the words of the Roman Governor, Festus found in Acts 25:19. He could not follow much of the debate between Paul and Paul's Jewish opponents, but he perceived that they disagreed "about a certain dead man, Jesus, whom Paul asserted to be alive." This point needs to be stressed today because many people relegate "matters of faith" to the realm of the irrational and subjective. In their mind faith is nothing like science or history where there are right and wrong answers. Some Christians even traffic in this kind of thinking, suggesting that people should "try Jesus, because even if it's not true you'll have a more peaceful and meaningful life." The Apostle Paul aggressively countered this line of thought. For him, the resurrection either happened or it didn't. If it did (as he believed), it changed everything. And if it did not then Christians were to be pitied because their life was a bad joke.

[10] This passage is taken from Luke 24. It would be wonderful to have a record of that explanation! Lacking that, I am including an excerpt from a sermon Tim Keller gave in which he highlights a number of the signs the disciples may have missed. "The light went on and they came to realize that David killing Goliath wasn't ultimately a call for us to defeat giants, it was an event that pointed ahead to Jesus, who would defeat the giants that can really kill us. They realized that Jesus was and is the true and better Adam, who passed the test in a much tougher Garden, and whose obedience is imputed to us. Jesus is the true and better Abel, who, though innocent, was slain and whose blood cries out, not for our condemnation but for our redemption. Jesus is the true and better Abraham, who answered God's call and left the comfort of the familiar to go into the void – a place not known – for us. Jesus is the true and better Isaac, who was not just offered up but who was sacrificed by his father. Jesus is the true and better Joseph, who was sold into slavery but who rose to sit at the right hand of power, and forgives those who sold him. Jesus is the true and better Moses, who stands in the gap between the Father and mankind and mediates a better covenant. Jesus is the true and better Esther, who didn't just risk losing an earthly position but lost a heavenly one, and didn't just risk his life but gave his life; who didn't just say, 'If I perish, I perish', but who said, 'when I perish I do so to save my people.' Jesus is the true and better Jonah, who was cast out from the boat into the storm so that we can be saved, and who survived three

days in the belly of the beast. Jesus is the true and better Passover Lamb. Jesus is the true and better Temple. Jesus is the true and better Prophet. Jesus is the true and better Priest." In so many ways, the Hebrew Scriptures point to Jesus. During the forty days between his resurrection and ascension, Christ explained who he was, why he had come and how the Old Testament had been pointing ahead to him.

[11] Acts 1:8f.

[12] The Ascension and Coronation of Christ – which was prophesied about by Daniel (Daniel 7:13f), David (Ps. 110:1-5) Isaiah (Is. 52:13) and Jesus (John 17) and referenced by Paul (Phil 2:5-11; Eph. 1) – not only let the disciples know that Christ's post-resurrection appearances were over, and made it clear that he had been exalted to the highest place, they also gave them a clear understanding of the resurrection body. Jesus did not rise as a spirit. He went into heaven in his body. The incarnation of the Son of Man was (and is) an eternal thing. He did not shed humanity at death or in his ascension. Though the Ascension is only mentioned twice in the New Testament, Christians in the early church considered the Thursday that fell forty days after Easter as one of the six most important days of the year.

[13] Jesus existed as God (the Logos) before he became the God-Man. During this time he enjoyed more glory and honor than we can imagine. At the incarnation he gave all of this up, agreeing to not simply become a man, or even a slave, but a slave who went to his death, "even death on a cross." Paul notes that Jesus became sin (2 Cor. 5:21) and that he bore the Father's wrath. No one ever went lower. As a result, the Father exalted him to the highest place – one even higher than he had previously enjoyed.

[14] A more complete explanation of the Holy Spirit lies outside the context of this study. Suffice it to say that, prior to Christ's ascension the Holy Spirit (the third member of the Trinity) empowered certain people at certain times (prophets, kings, etc), but after Pentecost he indwells every true believer, equipping and empowering them for the work he has called them to do. Part of growing in joy and faith is learning to yield more of our life to the Spirit of God.

[15] The church has not been perfect. In fact, she falls well short of her calling. However, acting together or alone, Christ's followers have been on the forefront of many of the best causes – e.g., starting hospitals, building orphanages, funding and staffing homeless shelters and founding schools and universities. Christians have championed labor rights, prison reform and public sanitation. It is popular to dismiss the church – or even bash it. But many historians report it to be one the most successful – if not the single

most – successful humanitarian and reform movement in history.

[16] At the moment of our death, our body and soul (spirit) separate. The first returns to dirt while the second either goes to a place of great joy or great sorrow. (The place of great joy is referred to as Paradise or Abraham's bosom but not Heaven. Likewise, the place of suffering is referred to as Hades or Sheol, but not hell. Heaven and hell are technically understood to be permanent locations where we are sent after judgment.) After Christ returns, our bodies will be renewed and reunited with our souls and in this new state we will stand ready for final judgment.

[17] There are two separate judgments. Those who have been justified through Christ are judged at the Judgment Seat of Christ (Rom. 14:10-12); those who stand outside of Christ are judged at the Great White Throne Judgment (Rev. 20:11-15). Every believer in Christ will give an account of himself, and the Lord will judge the decisions he made. This judgment does not determine salvation, which is by faith in Christ alone (Eph. 2:8-9). Rather, it is the time when believers will give an account of their lives in service to Christ (I Cor. 3:11-15). Those things we have done that honor God and reflect the values of Christ will yield "gold, silver and precious stones." The fire of God's judgment will burn up the "wood, hay and stubble" of the words we spoke and things we did which had no eternal value. The second judgment (The Great White Throne Judgment) is for unbelievers. This judgment does not determine salvation, either. Everyone at the Great White Throne is an unbeliever and therefore already doomed to be cut off from God. Those who stand alone – without Christ – will be judged on the basis of their works alone. All thoughts, words and actions will be judged against God's perfect standard and found wanting.

[18] There are those who refuse to discuss the empty tomb because they refuse to accept any part of the story as true. Some go so far as to deny that Jesus even existed. As I noted earlier, this is not a viable option. We not only have the record of the New Testament – one of the best attested ancient documents we have – we also have non-Christian sources that contend that: there was a first century prophet named Jesus who lived in the area of Palestine; he was esteemed for his wisdom and virtue; he was condemned for blasphemy and crucified under Pontius Pilate. There is enough information from "hostile witnesses" to establish all of this plus the fact that the Christian faith was born out of the belief that he had risen from the dead. Those who dismiss Jesus on the basis of too little evidence not only need to be prepared to write off Plato, Socrates, Homer and Virgil, they need to admit that they have less reason to believe in Genghis Khan, Alexander the Great, Joan of Arc, and Dante than they do in Christ.

[19] The historical arguments for the resurrection are significant and have per-

suaded many skeptics. Do not let this brief treatment deter you from more detailed explorations of this topic. In the 1930s Frank Morrison (a lawyer) set out to disprove the resurrection and in the end became persuaded that it was true. His book, Who Moved the Stone? (Faber & Faber, 1930) is considered a classic. More recently, another attorney – Yale-trained Lee Strobel – set out to do the same thing. Frustrated with his wife's decision to become a Christian, he set out to disprove the basis for her faith. In the process he also became a Christian. His book, The Case for Christ, chronicles his journey to faith. Many other books on the same topic are available as well, including Dr. William Lane Craig's The Son Rises: The Historical Evidence for the Resurrection of Jesus (Chicago: Moody, 1981); Gary Habermas and Anthony Flew, Did Jesus Rise from the Dead? The Resurrection Debate, ed. Terry Miethe (New York: Harper and Row, 1987), et al.

[20] There are variations on the Swoon Theory – e.g., Luke gave Jesus drugs that allowed him to fake his death; a secret society helped stage the event, etc. – but they all require us to assume that Jesus was able to survive the flogging and crucifixion.

[21] According to Merrill Tenney (The Reality of the Resurrection, Harper and Row, 1963), Jewish custom included washing and straightening the body and then bandaging it tightly from the armpits to the ankles in strips of linen about one foot wide. Aromatic spices, "often of a gummy consistency, were placed between the wrappings or folds." We are told that Joseph and Nicodemus treated the body with 75 pounds of aromatic spices. It seems unlikely that a healthy person could survive being mummified for more than five minutes, never mind a critically-injured one surviving for forty hours. (Merrill Tenney, The Reality of the Resurrection (New York: Harper and Row Publishers, 1963).

[22] One writer suggested that you set the following challenge in front of advocates of the Swoon Theory. "Let me beat you with a cat-o-nine tails for thirty-nine strokes, nail you to a cross, hang in the blistering sun for six hours, run a spear into your heart, embalm you and then set you in an airless tomb for a few days. After that we'll see how you are feeling." It makes the point. If you have doubts about the horrors of flogging, watch a few minutes of Mel Gibson's movie, The Passion of the Christ. Jesus was reduced to a bloody piece of meat. You can also review the basics of the crucifixion found in the previous study.

[23] The Gospel writers described what happened even though they did not know that medically-trained personnel would later affirm that this separation was a clear sign of death.

[24] Dr. John Blanchard notes that there have been more conspiracy theories

about the resurrection of Jesus Christ than about the assassination of John F. Kennedy. He goes on to note that while some of the Kennedy theories have a measure of credibility, the Swoon Theory has none. (Blanchard, Jesus: Dead or Alive, Darlington, England: EP Books, 2009), p. 11.

25 John Blanchard, Jesus: Dead or Alive, Darlington: EP, 2009, p. 17.

26 Mark 16:11

27 John 20:25

28 Mark 16:14

29 W.E. Vine, Expository Dictionary of New Testament Words.

30 Two different locations vie for the spot where Christ was buried: one is located at the Church of the Holy Sepulcher; the other is called the Garden Tomb. The Church of the Holy Sepulcher is located with the city walls (which are not the same walls as were present at the time of Christ). This location would not require a fifteen minute walk. The Garden Tomb is outside the city gates – but not far.

31 Andrew Fairbairn, Studies in the Life of Christ, cited in Blanchard, p. 13.

32 John 20:1-9; Lk 24:9-12

33 There are many powerful quotes to cite here. I will only include two. First, C.F.D. Moule: "From the very first, the conviction that Jesus had been raised from death has been that by which [the Christians'] very existence has stood or fallen. There was no other motive to account for them, to explain them... At no point within the New Testament is there any evidence that the Christians stood for an original philosophy of life or an original ethic. Their sole function is to bear witness to what they claim as an event – the raising of Jesus from among the dead... The one really distinctive thing for which the Christians stood was their declaration that Jesus had been raised from the dead according to God's design, and the consequent estimate of Him as in a unique sense Son of God and representative man, and the resulting conception of the way to reconciliation." Second: Dr. William Lane Craig, an author with two earned Ph.Ds. (one in philosophy and one in history) writes: "Without the belief in the Resurrection the Christian faith could not have come into being. The disciples would have remained crushed and defeated men. Even had they continued to remember Jesus as their beloved teacher, His crucifixion would have forever silenced any hopes of His being the Messiah. The cross would have remained the sad and shameful end of His career. The origin of Christianity therefore hinges on the belief of the

early disciples that God had raised Jesus from the dead."

34 Charles Colson, Kingdoms in Conflict, Hodder & Stoughton, p. 70.

35 "Had the crucifixion of Jesus ended His disciples' experience of Him, it is hard to see how the Christian Church could have come into existence. The Church was founded on faith in the Messiahship of Jesus. A crucified Messiah was no Messiah at all. He was one rejected by Judaism and accursed by God. It was the Resurrection of Jesus, as St. Paul describes in Romans 1:4, which proclaimed Him to be the Son of God with power." H.D.A. Major

36 One of the early opponents of the Christian faith was the second-century Greek philosopher, Celsus. One of the arguments he put forward against the resurrection unfolded as follows, "Christianity cannot be true because the written accounts of the resurrection are based on the testimony of women, and we all know that women are hysterical."

37 If someone had fabricated the resurrection they would have chosen a man to be the first to see the risen Christ. Indeed, it is likely that they would have had a prominent man witness the resurrection itself. As it is, no one actually sees the resurrection occur, and women are the first to talk with Jesus after he rose.

38 Mark 16:5; Luke 24:4 and Matthew 28:2f.

39 The discrepancies are quickly reconcilable to those who've studied history. Were they angels or men? Angels. Men "dressed in white robes" or "in clothes that gleam like lightening" are angels, not men. Were there one or two? There were two. Mark only mentions one, but he does not say "only one."

40 Even Christ's enemies acknowledged that he predicted his death and resurrection. See: Mt. 27:63. See also Mk 8:31; Mt. 17:22 and Luke 9:22.

41 It's unthinkable that a group of liars would remain loyal to one another and die for their lie in poverty and disgrace. The radical change in their lives makes it clear; they believed Jesus was God. Simon Greenleaf, a professor at Harvard Law School and an expert on legal evidence, wrote, "it's impossible that they could have persisted in affirming the truths they have narrated, had Jesus not actually risen from the dead, and had they not known this fact as certainly as they knew any other fact." Simon Greenleaf, The Testimony of the Evangelists: The Gospels Examined by the Rules of Evidence Administered in Courts of Justice (Grand Rapids, MI: Kregel, 1995), p. 32. First cited in Vintage Jesus, Mark Driscoll (Wheaton: Crossway, 2007), p. 135.

[42] Our culture has wrongly divided fact and faith – suggesting that fields like science and finance traffic in the first, while religion and spirituality are based entirely on the second. This is not true. Indeed, I believe the case for faith in Christ is overwhelming.

CHAPTER 6
Ten Questions

I believe in Christianity as I believe that the sun has risen: not only because I see it,
but because by it I see everything else.
C.S. Lewis

Jesus went to Jerusalem to announce the Good News to the people of that city. And
Jesus knew that he was going to put a choice before them: will you be my disciple,
or will you be my executioner? There is no middle ground here. Jesus went to
Jerusalem to put people in a situation where they had to say yes or no.
Henri Nouwen

Life is full of questions. So is the Christian faith. Some of these questions get answered. Some fall away. A few come up over and over. In the pages that follow I attempt to answer ten of the most common questions that emerge from a study of Christ's life.

One: What did Jesus teach?

Jesus spent a lot of time explaining the Scriptures, telling stories and teaching people. What exactly did he teach? What was his message? Theologians divide the study of Christ into three separate disciplines: his life, his work and his teaching. We've been focused on the first two. It's worth spending a couple pages on the third. Jesus was a rabbi. What exactly did he teach? What was the essence of his message?

Before I share my summary let me make two points. First, hundreds of thousands of books – and tens of millions of sermons – have attempted to answer this question. All of them fail. None of them contain the raw power of Christ's own words. My efforts will also fall short. So let me make a suggestion: why not read Christ's words yourself? Everything he said fits on twenty typed pages, which is far less than you'll find in today's USA Today. You can read them in less than an hour. Take this challenge. Find a red-letter Bible, strap yourself into your chair and begin. But be warned: whitewater rafting trips are more relaxing. The words of the Word are among the most riveting, alarming, comforting and shocking known to mankind. Most people are unprepared. Some suffer whiplash.

Second, the central focus of Christ's teaching was Christ himself. Both what he did and what he said reinforced his claim to be the Way, the Truth and the Life. In one sense it would be fair to say that Jesus was his own most frequent subject.

However, we would be infinitely poorer if we did not celebrate the ethical system Christ set before us. Even those who do not worship Jesus as God frequently recognize him as the greatest moral teacher of all time. Between the Sermon on the Mount, the Golden Rule and his selfless example, he laid out a path that would lead to world peace if it were ever universally embraced. It is based on five assumptions.

- **God Comes First:** Most of us love ourselves first, family members second and God third. Jesus reversed the order. He instructed us to love our Heavenly Father with all of our heart, soul, mind and strength. Indeed, he called on us to love God with such fierce passion that our love for our own family would look like hatred beside it.[2] In Christ's ethic, God is preeminent. He does not exist for our own glory; we exist for his. He is first.

- **Others Are Second.** Christ's teaching moved from a command to love God to a command to love others, especially the poor. People matter. Our vertical focus on God is expected to overflow into horizontal acts of mercy, justice, reconciliation and service. Feelings alone are not enough. Jesus went so far as to demand that we care for those we hate.[3]

- **The Way Up Is Down.** Jesus announced that "the first shall be last," those who "seek to save their life will lose it" and that those who really want to get ahead will wash the dirty feet of those around them. These were not commands to act against our own best interests, but statements designed to correct our confusion and selfish bias. In God's economy the way up really is down.[4]

- **We Are Going To Live Forever**. According to Jesus, we will either spend eternity with God in a place of love and joy, or we will be eternally cut off from all that is gracious and good. This truth affects everything. In fact, little of what Christ said makes sense unless we look past the grave and into the world to come. Jesus taught that those who focus only on this life are fools.

- **We Are Stewards.** Finally, Christ grounded his ethical system on the belief that everything we "own" is on loan from God, and that we are expected to "invest" his resources in ways that reflect his priorities. He made much of the idea that we will be held accountable for what we do with what is entrusted to us. He also stressed that those to whom much has been given will be held to a higher standard.

There is a beautiful simplicity to Christ's teaching. Anyone can make things complicated. Few can make the complicated simple. Jesus explained graduate-level moral concepts in ways preschoolers could grasp, and he did so without being simplistic.

Two: Why did the Jews reject Jesus?

If Jesus was the Jewish Messiah – and the Jews had been waiting for centuries for him to arrive – why did they reject him?

There are a number of issues wrapped up in this question. Let me break them apart and take them one at a time.

First, why does anyone reject Jesus? If there is so much evidence that he is God, why doesn't everyone – both Jew and Gentile – see it and accept him?

If you ask people who do not believe in Christ to answer this question you hear a number of things. Some argue that there is no evidence to support his claims. Others talk about a bad experience at church, a dislike for organized religion or a belief that all Christians are hypocrites. Still others say that they have a hard time believing in a God of love given all the things that are going wrong in the world. A final group indicates that they are willing to believe in Jesus, just not yet. They want to have "a bit of fun first."

If you turn to the Bible for an answer, you find a very different list. In the Parable of the Four Soils, Jesus suggested that some people have hard hearts, others are distracted by the concerns of the world, and still others are overwhelmed by sin. In Romans 1 the Apostle Paul argues that there is plenty of evidence that God exists for those who are open to it, but he reports that many "suppress the truth" because of their wickedness. In Romans 10 he adds that some people do not believe in Christ because no one told them about him.[5] Clearly there is not one single reason.

Why did his Jewish contemporaries reject him? *If Jesus was the fulfillment of their prophecies, and if they were anxious for their Messiah to arrive, then why didn't they put two and two together? Why didn't they recognize and embrace him?*

The first point that needs to be made is that many did accept Jesus as the Messiah. The early church was comprised entirely of Jews. Every one of the twelve disciples was Jewish, and some of Christ's earliest followers were even Pharisees. The second point is that many of them rejected him for the same reasons many reject him today – they have a hard heart, are enticed by sin or haven't really heard his claims. However there were two other reasons that really got in the way.

- **He was very different than they expected.** Most first-century Jews thought their biggest problem was Rome. Consequently, they read the prophecies in ways that suggested that the Messiah would be a political-military leader who would secure their freedom and bring back the glory days of Israel. Jesus was unwilling to do this. He understood his assignment to be much bigger than their temporal and regional concerns. Indeed, his goal was nothing less than blessing the entire world.

- **Their leaders lined up against him.** A second reason the people did not embrace Jesus is because many of their leaders campaigned against him. Some of these men were jealous of the large crowds that turned out to hear Jesus speak. Others hated him because of the harsh things he said about them.[6] Still others were horrified by his claims to be God. The point is, the religious leaders of the day saw Jesus not as their Messiah, but as a dangerous radical. Consequently, rather than pointing people to him, they pointed people away.

Why do Jews continue to reject Christ? Over the last 2,000 years there has been plenty of time for Jewish people to see that God's plan was different than they thought and embrace him as their Messiah. Why haven't they done so?

Once again, the question needs to be modified to recognize that many do embrace Christ as Lord, and that many of those who do not, do not for the same reasons many Gentiles do not. It also should be stressed that many contemporary Jews are just as unfamiliar with the ways Christ fulfilled their prophecies as many Gentiles are.[7] However, there are two other issues that have developed over time. Many twenty-first century Jews reject Christ because of the anti-Semitism that has riddled the church through the years. Others hesitate to consider his claims because to do so would be perceived as an act of betrayal against their family.[8]

Three: Is Jesus really the only way to God?

The Bible seems to suggest that Jesus is the only way to God and that all other religions are wrong. This is not just harsh it's dangerous! Do you really expect me to believe in a God who is so narrow-minded? Why can't Christians be more tolerant?

Many people are willing to believe that Jesus is special. Some are even willing to affirm that everything he claimed about himself is true... except the idea that he is the only way to God. Is this really the claim? Is Jesus the only way to gain eternal life?

One: This is the claim. In the Sermon on the Mount, Jesus argued that there is a popular trail that leads away from God and a road less traveled that leads towards him. He then contended that many will be led astray by false prophets who claim to speak for God. Additionally, he boldly proclaimed, "I am the way, the truth and the life. No one gets to the Father except through me."

In making this exclusive claim, Jesus endorsed what was taught in the Old Testament before him and the New Testament after him.[9] This does not mean that his claims are true – we are always free to disagree. But we need to acknowledge that both the Bible in general and Jesus in particular claim that Jesus is the only way to a right relationship with God.

Two: This claim has never been popular. The "one way to God" argument is not popular today. It's worth noting that it has never been popular. Christians were not fed to the lions for believing in Jesus; they were fed to the lions for believing "only in Jesus." Roman authorities would have been fine with Christians announcing that Jesus was "a god," as long as they also declared that Caesar was "a god." It was the exclusive claims of Christ that got them in trouble.

Of course truth is not determined by popular acclaim. It's always possible that the majority is wrong. The question we ultimately need to be concerned with is not, "What is popular?" but "What is true?"

Three: Everyone has exclusive beliefs. In today's world, about the worst thing that can be said about you is that you are intolerant. Ironically, the most intolerant people are often those forcing tolerance on others, while failing to see that their belief in tolerance is itself an exclusive belief.

Let me be quick to admit that exclusive claims of any sort – including the exclusive claims made by Christians! – can lead to trouble. People who believe that they alone are right, or (worse yet) that they have God on their side, often end up feeling superior to those of differing beliefs. This can spiral into some sort of marginalization or even oppression of others. Clearly, we need to display more care and humility than we often do. However, it's also imperative that we understand that everyone is making these claims. Those who say there is one way to God and those who say all paths are equally valid are both making un-provable, exclusive claims of truth.

Today it is considered open-minded to assert that "all religions are equally true," or that "every religion sees part of the truth but none see the whole," or that "it's arrogant to claim that your religion is superior to others." However, each of these "open-minded" claims is actually an exclusive claim. People who say, "It's arrogant to claim that any one view is true," are arrogantly claiming that their view is true.

Yes, Jesus makes exclusive claims. But so does everyone else.

Four: The differences between religions are real. Some people contend that all the major religions are essentially alike – that is, though there are superficial differences between them, they all basically promote the same idea and ideals.[10] This is not true. Once you start comparing the tenets of various religions you realize that it's the similarities that are superficial and the differences that are overwhelming.

This does not deny that there is truth in every religion, nor suggest that different religions do not overlap in some ways. It does not suggest that people do not have the right to believe what they wish.[11] However, the differences are real.

- Jews argue that there is only one God, Hindus contend there are millions and most Buddhists deny that there are any. Do these views sound compatible to you?

- Hindus believe that a person advances through a series of reincarnations until they work through their karma and meld into a single cosmic consciousness. Christians teach that we are born once, live once and die once, after which we face judgment and then exist in an eternity where we will forever remain uniquely who we are. The differences between these two views are not superficial.

- Muslims do not believe that Jesus is God or that he rose from the dead. Christians say he is fully God and that he did rise. Both cannot be right. [12]

I could go on, but you get the point. Far from being essentially the same, the major religions disagree on the nature of reality, the nature of God and the purpose of man. They disagree on the essence of our problem(s) and how they are fixed. They have radically different understandings of what is expected of us and what happens when we die. The only logical conclusion you can reach after you compare them is that, while they might all be wrong, they cannot all be right. [13]

Five: Sincerity is not a valid test for truth. There is a second group of people who take a different approach. They acknowledge that significant differences between religions exist, but insist that all are equally valid. Some in this camp go so far as to suggest that you are free to believe whatever you want because "anything goes and everything works as long as you are sincere."[14] The problem is that sincerity is not a test for truth.

Think about it. Is there any area of life other than religion where you believe we are free to make up our own truth? Would you go to a doctor who thought this way? Would you trust a banker who "sincerely believed" that 1 + 1 = 23? And if you do believe that sincerity is a test of truth, what would you say to the person who sincerely believes that salvation comes through sacrificing infants, or who sincerely believes the sincerity test is wrong?

I understand the appeal of suggesting that every religious belief is true, especially in a world where religion has turned violent. After all, if anything you believe is true and everything works, then there is no reason to try to convert anyone. Everyone should take a stress pill and join in singing "Live and let live." But we need to deal with reality.[15] All people have equal worth, but all ideas do not.[16] Just because we believe something is true does not mean that it is. Those who believe that "anything you believe is true and everything works" are not even engaged in wishful thinking, they are engaged in wishing.

Six: The Claims of Christ are Unique: I am not suggesting that the Christian faith is better because Christians are better – i.e., more moral, spiritual or intellectually astute than people of other faiths. What I am suggesting is that the Christian faith is unique because it rests on the person and work of Christ – and Jesus was unique. No one else lived a perfect life. No one else fulfilled the law. No one else fulfilled the Messianic prophecies. No one else died as the perfect sacrifice. No one else rose from the dead. No other major religious figure has claimed to be God.

At the end of the day, other religions claim that you are reconciled with God on the basis of your good works. Christianity says that we are saved only on the basis of the works of another, namely Christ. This is unique.
Seven: You Have to Make a Decision. You have to land the plane. You have to place your bets. It's time to fish or cut bait. Select your cliché of choice. They all work. Just be sure to move forward. No one who thinks carefully about what is at stake thinks that hanging out in no-man's-land is a wise choice. If you haven't resolved this issue, make it your highest priority. Let me humbly suggest that deciding what you believe about ultimate matters – God, eternity, etc. – is a bit more important than watching a second hour of ESPN.

Four: Are we really expected to believe in the Virgin Birth?

Mary was not the first young woman to get "in trouble" and start telling stories. But we all know where babies come from. And we know that virgins don't get pregnant. Why do some people insist on holding onto the Virgin Birth? Is it really necessary to believe in it to be a Christian?

We do know where babies come from. But unless we are prepared to write off miracles altogether, I do not understand why this particular one causes so much angst. Or, to state this differently, having already made peace with the idea that God is the Creator, I do not see why the Virgin Birth presents any problems.[17] Additionally, I believe there are at least four strong reasons we need to affirm this doctrine.[18]

One: The Old Testament Prophecies: The claim that a virgin will conceive does not begin with Mary, it's introduced in Genesis 3. There, as God is rendering a curse upon the serpent, He says:

> "Because you have done this, cursed are you more than all cattle, and more than every beast of the field; On your belly you will go, and dust you will eat all the days of your life; And I will put enmity between you and the woman, and between your seed and her seed; He shall bruise you on the head, and you shall bruise him on the heel." [19]

This passage is enormously important for a half dozen reasons. At the moment I only ask that you see one thing: in this announcement God refers to Jesus as "her seed."
I will put enmity between you and the woman, and between your seed and her seed.

The Hebrew term that is used here is zera. It is also translated sperm. As anyone who has passed Intro to Biology knows, women do not have sperm. Males have sperm. Females have eggs. So, why would God have referred to Jesus as "the seed of woman" except to announce that the One he was sending would not have a human father.[20]

Isaiah 7:14 contains a second Old Testament reference to the Virgin Birth. In this passage, which was written 700 years before Christ was born, we read:

> *Therefore the Lord himself will give you a sign: The virgin will be with child and will give birth to a son, and he will call him, Immanuel (God with us).*[21]

The first reason we should affirm the Virgin Birth is because it was quietly implied and boldly prophesied about hundreds of years before Christ was born.

Two: The New Testament Gospels: The Virgin Birth of Christ is highlighted by two of the Gospel writers. The first to do so is Matthew, a tax collector by trade. It seems reasonable to assume that in that role he learned how to keep accurate records. The second person to report the virgin conception was Luke, a physician who would have been professionally inclined to doubt such a claim; instead he supports it. [22]

Three: Christ's ability to be the Savior requires a unique birth. If Jesus had a human father, then he would have contracted the same sinful nature common to everyone else, and as a sinner he would be unqualified to atone for anyone else's sin.[23]   He would have had to die to pay his own debts instead.

Four: Christ was unique. The Bible does not claim that a normal person was conceived by a virgin; it suggests that the eternal son of God was. Jesus' life did not begin at conception. He existed before Creation as God. He entered time and space through a virgin's womb in order to add humanity to divinity. It makes sense that his birth would be unique.
If you are going to take out a red pen and start drawing lines through things outside your experience, you will end up crossing out some very critical parts of Scripture. And what is left will not hold together. For starters, the most unbelievable concept in the Bible is not the Virgin Birth, it's that God was willing to become a man in the first place.

Having made these points let me return to the original question: Is belief in the Virgin Birth 'necessary' to be a Christian? Well, that depends on exactly what is being asked. Can someone place their faith in Christ and be born again without understanding the unique nature of his birth? Certainly. This would describe most children who come to faith. But the real question is, can someone deny the Virgin Birth and be a Christian? That is more vexing.

The question reminds me of one I heard posed some time ago: How much can you remove from a car and still call it a car? If you take the headlights off is it still a car? Sure. What about the bumpers? Yes. What about the body? OK. And if we remove the tires as well, is it still a car without a body or tires? Yes, I think so, but it's not going anywhere. What about the engine? Do you call a frame without a body, tires or engine a car?[24] I don't think so.

My experience is that anyone who insists on denying the Virgin Birth will want to deny enough other critical components so that what is left is also not going anywhere. Denying the Virgin Birth not only discredits the Old and New Testaments and the earliest creeds, it also undermines the incarnation and Christ's sinless status.[25] I'm not really sure what would be left to affirm. The salvation we seek comes our way only through a virgin-born God-Man.

Five: What about the "other" Gospels?

This study of Christ's life was based on Matthew, Mark, Luke and John – the four Gospels found in the New Testament. But in recent years a number of other gospels have been discovered that have a different slant on Christ. They provide us with new information. Why are you ignoring them?

The short answer is, the "new Gospels" are not new discoveries; they are old fakes that were dismissed years ago for good reason. The longer answer requires a bit of background. In fact, in order to understand why certain books do not appear in the canon,[26] you have to understand why others do. Let's start at the beginning.

The Bible is a collection of books. As I noted in a previous study, one way to think about the Bible is as a compilation of sixty-six books that were written over sixteen-hundred years by forty different authors in three languages and on three continents.

The thirty-nine books that comprise the Hebrew Bible (i.e., the Old

Testament) are a cross section of historical books, prophetic works and wisdom literature. These were written over the course of one thousand years, completed by 400 B.C. and in wide circulation in the Jewish world by the first century. These books were then adopted as a package by the church, in large part because of the endorsement of Jesus himself.

The twenty-seven books that constitute the New Testament – which is comprised of the story of Christ's life (the Gospels), the story of the early church (the Book of Acts), a series of letters to various people and churches (the Epistles), and the Book of Revelation – were written between 45 and 95 A.D.

The Bible is a collection of inspired books. A second way to think about the Bible is as a letter from God. Everything we know about the Creator we know because he revealed it to us through one of two means: natural (also called general) revelation or supernatural (also called special) revelation.

- Natural revelation refers to the things we can learn about the Creator by studying the creation. David refers to this in Psalm 19 when he speaks about the stars revealing the glory of God.

- Supernatural revelation refers to the "beyond nature" ways that God discloses himself to us. The most powerful example of this is Jesus himself. As the writer of Hebrews notes, "The Son is the radiance of God's glory and the exact representation of his being."[27] If you want to know what God is like, just look at the Son. But there is a second way in which God supernaturally reveals himself, and that is the Bible. The Holy Spirit worked through human authors to provide us with a God-authored book.[28]

The New Testament did not fall from the sky in its present form. The twenty-seven books that comprise the New Testament did not arrive as a package, complete with chapter divisions, verses and maps in the back. It came together in a multistep process.

First, as noted above, God inspired various leaders (mostly Apostles) to write books and letters that revealed his nature, Christ's life, the rescue plan, how we should live, etc. The Holy Spirit directed this process to ensure that the right words made it onto the page.

Second, God inspired the church to ensure that the right pages made it into the Book. This process began when the author of the first New Testament document – likely James or Paul – picked up a quill and started writing, but it was not finalized until the fourth century. Let me explain.

After a letter (or Gospel) was written, copies were made and put into circulation.[29] They joined a variety of other books and letters that were being passed from one person to the next and read at church services and other gatherings. This material sorted itself into four categories.

- The works of the Apostles themselves – i.e., the Gospels of Matthew and John, the letters of Peter, Paul, James and John. These were immediately accepted.

- The books written by authors closely associated with an apostle – i.e., the Gospels of Mark and Luke. These were quickly accepted.

- Letters written by godly people offering wise advice but lacking any apostolic connections. These were appreciated but eventually rejected.

- Letters written by those advocating aberrant views, with a few of these being passed off as the work of one of the apostles themselves – e.g., The Gospel of Thomas. These were also rejected.

It's important to realize that the early church leaders did not bestow authority on certain books (or withhold it from others), they simply sought to discern which books were from God. To that end they asked three questions: first, which letters had the self-authenticating voice of God; second, which letters were proving helpful to Christians; and finally, which letters were tied to an Apostle.

The New Testament canon was in place in the fourth century. In 367 A.D. – shortly after Constantine passed the Edict of Milan lifting the ban on Christianity throughout the Roman Empire and allowing Christian leaders to meet openly for the first time in nearly three hundred years – Athanasius published a list of New Testament books. It is the same list we recognize today. This list was not the result of a formal vote. It simply reflected the consensus that had emerged over the previous two hundred years.

The "new gospels" are not new. A few years ago Dan Brown's best-selling book, The DaVinci Code, focused attention on The Gospel of Judas. In the novel – which Brown claimed was based on fact – various characters argued that Judas' Gospel, along with close to eighty others, had been kept out of the canon by the disciples. The specific charge was that they had been suppressed in the disciples' effort to cling to power. This claim made for great headlines and sold a lot of books. But there are two big problems with it:

- **First, the "new gospels" are not new.** In spite of Brown's suggestion that these works have only recently been discovered, scholars have known about them for hundreds of years. They have been studied, exposed as frauds, mined for insights of any type and then set aside. They have not garnered a lot of popular press because they were understood not to have much to offer.

- **Second, the "new gospels" are not old.** Or, to be more precise, they are not old enough to matter. In spite of claims to the contrary, the main reason they were not included when the canon was being shaped is because they were not around![30] They certainly do not have any unique insights about Christ because they were written by people who lived long after he was crucified.

If you have any doubts, read the "new gospels" for yourself. If you are concerned that you might be missing out on something – or that there has been a secret, two-thousand-year-old cover-up – then by all means, read them for yourself. Many are available online. I am quite confident that you will quickly see why they have been set aside. My only request is, read the real Gospels first! If you want to know about Jesus, you can never do better than to read Matthew, Mark, Luke and John.

Six: If Christ is King why are so many things going wrong?

Earlier you stated that Jesus now sits at the right hand of the Father and has ultimate power and authority. Well, if that is true, then why is the world such a mess? Why are there wars, earthquakes and tsunamis? Why do children suffer in poverty and abuse? Why is there cancer, injustice, divorce and heartache? If Christ is a good and powerful King, why are so many things going wrong?

The classic statement of this problem was coined by the ancient Greek philosopher, Epicurus. He wrote:

> Either God wants to abolish evil and he cannot. Or he can but he does not want to. Or he cannot and does not want to. If he wants to but cannot, he is impotent. If he can and does not, he is wicked. But if God both can and wants to abolish evil, then how come evil is in the world. [31]

Let me start by acknowledging that I am not able to fully answer this question. Many have tried, but a definitive answer lies beyond our present reach. More importantly, let me say that I am very sorry for those of you who are hurting right now. What you need is a good friend to sit with you, not someone's dispassionate attempt to explain why things are still going wrong. [32]

But there is a need for us to think carefully about this question. Though a full answer eludes us, some helpful things can be said.

One: The world is broken because of our sin. Many people ask, "Why didn't God create a world where tragedy and suffering did not exist?" The answer is: He did! In Genesis 1:31 we are told that, "God saw all that he had made and it was very good." The problem is that He gave us options.

God wanted us to experience love. That cannot be forced. Love always involves a choice.[33] We abused that choice and as a result everything broke. Our sin infected and affected everything, leaving us to live in "the long melancholy aftermath of a primordial catastrophe." [34] The Bible is very clear that God is not the author of sin or evil. He created a world that had the potential for evil – and foresaw what would follow – but the blame for sin and suffering rests with us.

Two: God can use our suffering to accomplish good. Some of what looks horrible right now will look different later on. Let me be clear, some of what looks horrible at the moment is truly horrible. It's evil and wrong. God has allowed it to happen but he has not caused it, nor does he call it good.

But some of what we think of as bad today we will later recognize as good. The death of Christ is an example. Imagine being one of his disciples. You had the opportunity to listen to him teach and to watch him heal the sick. He befriended outcasts and served the poor. He was full of wisdom and grace. In so many different ways he was the perfect man. And then he was tragically and unjustly murdered.

Can you imagine thinking that his death was a good thing? No! The death of Christ would have struck you as the worst possible news. In fact, you might have thought, "There is no way I can ever follow a god who would allow this to happen."

Only later do you realize that Christ's death was actually the greatest thing that could ever happen, for it was only through Christ's death that you could be reconciled to God.

Not everything makes sense in real time. Right now we look at the backside of the tapestry. It is often impossible to see the pattern that will emerge. But the Bible is clear; God is ultimately in control, and many of the things we believe are horrible will be used for good.

Three: God is patiently holding back judgment and justice. One day suffering will end and God will judge evil. He will follow this by making all things new again! The promise for those who are in Christ is that we will eventually enjoy life at an entirely new level. But until that time we will suffer headaches and heartaches of all sorts. Jesus told us to expect it.[35]

Why can't things be good now? Why can't God stop evil and end pain today? The answer might surprise you – this might be your fault! To understand why, you need to realize two things. First, we cannot have it both ways. We cannot have a world of choices and a world free of pain at the same time, because some choices lead to pain! For that matter, it's unrealistic to think that God could step in and make things right without fundamentally overhauling your life. We want God to punish those who cause others to suffer without stopping to think how many times we are the ones causing the pain. God has promised that one day he will return and make things right. But at that point the show is over. The curtain falls and judgment follows. We can't have it both ways – this life and perfect life.

Which leads to the second point - God does not want to act until as many people place their faith in him as possible. In 2 Peter 3 we read the following:

> But do not forget this one thing, dear friends: With the Lord a day is like a thousand years, and a thousand years are like a day. The Lord is not slow in keeping his promise, as some understand slowness. *Instead he is patient with you, not wanting anyone to perish, but everyone to come to repentance.*

God is holding off so that people have a chance to choose eternal life over eternal death.

Four: God is not immune to your pain. Finally, there is one other very important thing you need to know: God understands your pain. He knows what it is like to suffer.

Some people will tell you that your pain is not real, and that the way forward is to ignore it. Others will acknowledge that your pain is real, and will promise you that it will end when you die. A third group argues that pain is real, but says that you need to rise above it anyway. God's first response is to say that he understands. Jesus Christ was like us in every way except sin. He faced every temptation we face. He took all our pain upon himself. He understands. In Christ you have a sympathetic high priest.

This does not immediately make things right, but it does help. And it also reframes the question. We begin to stop asking, "How can I trust a God who allows bad things to happen?" and learn to start asking, "How can I not trust a God who sent his own Son to die in my place?"

Seven: What did Jesus look like?

The oldest available images we have of Christ are from the fifth century. So, the short answer to this question is that we do not know what Jesus looked like. But several important things can be said.

First: He looked like everyone else. When Jesus added humanity to deity, he became a real person. He was fully human not merely human. That means you couldn't pick him out of a line up because of his halo and wings. He was not an angel or an abstraction; he was a real person, flesh and blood.

Second: He did not look like you. Unless you are a fit, thirty-year-old Jewish male with calloused hands and some muscles on your frame, Jesus did not look like you do today. I mention this because some people seem to think otherwise. I've seen pictures of an African Jesus, an Anglo Jesus, a Korean Jesus and a Chinese Jesus. I've even seen pictures of a female Jesus. None of these images are valid. Jesus was a Jewish male who spent most of his life working as a carpenter. Unless you fit that general description, he did not look like you.

Third: He probably did not look like your mental picture of him. I could be wrong, but here's the challenge. Many of us have an image of Jesus that has been shaped by the pictures we've seen or the movies we've watched. But in the fifty mainstream films made about Christ, none have used a Jewish actor, and many of the most popular pictures of Jesus are based on some false assumptions.

Many artists give Jesus long hair because they confuse the Nazirite vow – which prevented a person from cutting their hair – with being a Nazarene – which describes a person living in Nazareth. Jesus was the second not the first. Given the customs of the day, it's unlikely he had long hair.

Other artists, like Warner Salman – whose 1940s painting of Jesus sold three million copies in the first two years – portray Christ with feathered hair and delicate, almost feminine, features. Still others make him appear as though he'd never smile or give him perfect teeth.

We need to take a step back from all of this. The Gospels do not tell us what Jesus looked like, but they tell us enough about him and his world to give us a picture. They describe a man who performed his first miracle at a wedding, gained a reputation for gluttony,[36] and spent time with tax collectors, lepers and prostitutes. We know that he spent three years on the road, lived in a hot and dusty land, walked for miles at a time and spent his last three years hanging out with a dozen, thirty-something blue collar workers. Based on this it seems unlikely that Jesus was anything other than a man's man. He was lean, had strong hands, a quick smile, piercing eyes and a unique talent for leading men. He could be both tender and fearless.[37] He likely used nicknames and played practical jokes.

It's hard to think about Jesus without some kind of image coming to mind. It's important that this mental picture be shaped as much as possible by the information we are given in the Gospels.

Eight: Wasn't Christ's death a form of cosmic child abuse?

If Jesus was innocent then it's unthinkable that he was unjustly punished for our sin. The idea that the Father poured out his wrath on the Son seems barbaric. It's cosmic child abuse.

We are absolutely right in thinking that there was something horrific about Christ suffering on the cross in our place. Both the sacrifice he made and the suffering he endured are without parallel in human history.

Additionally, we are absolutely right to think that something horrific happened between the Father and the Son when Jesus hung on the cross. The tear that occurred between them – albeit a temporary one – was real. Christ's cry from the cross, "My God, My God why have you forsaken me?" came out of an existential agony so dark we cannot begin to grasp it.[38]

But it's wrong to think that what happened was some form of child abuse. To understand why, we need to be clear about three things:

First: Jesus willingly laid down his life. Christ did not go to the cross as a child; he went as a grown man and as the infinite God of the universe. At the time of the incarnation Jesus willingly laid aside the independent use of his divine attributes to come to earth to rescue us. He did so knowing that his mission would result in his death. Yes, God the Father put Christ forward to atone for our sin. But Jesus was very clear that no one was taking his life from him. Instead, he was laying it down for us.[39] The portrayal of the Father as the abuser and Jesus as the victim is not accurate or helpful. Christ was not an unwilling victim; he was a humble participant in the amazing grace God showered on this world.

Second: the Father did not act in irate anger. The Triune God of grace was motivated by love, not anger. The church has always rejected the idea that the Father – or the God of the Old Testament – is a God of wrath and vengeance, while Jesus is a God of love. Almost everything about that framework is wrong. Rather, God-in-three persons worked together for our salvation. He did not inflict pain on someone else; he lovingly absorbed it into himself.

God became human and offered his life-blood so that one day he could destroy all evil without destroying us.

Third, we are the ones who caused Christ to suffer. Finally, if you want to look at who is to blame for the horrors inflicted upon Christ, the Bible is quite clear about who you should blame. You'll find that person staring back at you every time you look in the mirror. at you every time you look in the mirror.

Our sin must be punished, and God lovingly and willingly absorbed the punishment that we rightly deserved.

Nine: When is Jesus going to return?

Every so often I hear someone say that Jesus is about to return. Some even give a date. But then that date comes and goes and life marches on. Is Jesus coming back or not? Why do some people think he is? And if he is, when?

Christ promised to return. Speculation about the timeline has been a topic of conversation for almost 2,000 years. Those who claim to know grab a lot of headlines, but to date they've always been wrong. Here is a quick overview of what we can say.

Jesus will come again. Jesus told his followers that he was going ahead to prepare a place for them, and that at the appropriate time he would return to take them (us) there. This promise is further developed in the writings of Peter, Paul and John. In fact, by some estimates, almost every New Testament book refers to Christ's return, as do many of the early creeds. You can be certain that the one who came as a child will come again as the King and Judge.

We do not know when. We know that Jesus will return. We know that it will be personal and visible. We know that it will be in triumph. We know that when he comes he will roll out his kingdom in a whole new way. What we do not know is when this will occur. In fact, in Matthew 24 Jesus is quite explicit about this.

But about that day or hour no one knows, not even the angels in heaven, nor the Son but only the Father. As it was in the days of Noah, so it will be at the coming of the Son of Man. For in the days before the flood, people were eating and drinking, marrying and giving in marriage, up to the day Noah entered the ark; and they knew nothing about what would happen until the flood came and took them all away. That is how it will be at the coming of the Son of Man. Two men will be in the field; one will be taken and the other left. Two women will be grinding with a hand mill; one will be taken and the other left.

Therefore keep watch, because you do not know on what day your Lord will come. But understand this: If the owner of the house had known at what time of night the thief was coming, he would have kept watch and would not have let his house be broken into. So you also must be ready, because the Son of Man will come at an hour when you do not expect him.

Given the clarity with which Jesus announced that "no one knows," it seems best to back away from those who say that they do.

There are three different understandings of the future. A lot of the discussion about Christ's return hinges on the opening verses in Revelation 20:

And I saw an angel coming down out of heaven, having the key to the Abyss and holding in his hand a great chain. He seized the dragon, that ancient serpent, who is the devil, or Satan, and bound him for a thousand years. He threw him into the Abyss, and locked and sealed it over him, to keep him from deceiving the nations anymore until the thousand years were ended. After that, he must be set free for a short time.

I saw thrones on which were seated those who had been given authority to judge. And I saw the souls of those who had been beheaded because of their testimony about Jesus and because of the word of God. They had not worshiped the beast or its image and had not received its mark on their foreheads or their hands. They came to life and reigned with Christ a thousand years. (The rest of the dead did not come to life until the thousand years were ended.) This is the first resurrection. Blessed and holy are those who share in the first resurrection. The second death has no power over them, but they will be priests of God and of Christ and will reign with him for a thousand years.

There are three different interpretations of this passage. Some believe that Christ will return after a thousand-year peaceful reign on earth. This position – which is called Postmillennialism – was popular in the early days of the church, but has fallen out of favor over time.[40] A second position – called Amillennialism – interprets the 1,000 year reign of Christ symbolically; they believe it is happening even now in heaven. A third group – the Premillennial position – believes that after Christ returns he will establish his kingdom on earth for 1,000 years. Within this third position there are different views based on alternate understandings of passages in the Book of Daniel, I Thessalonians and elsewhere.

I could go into much more detail here. Suffice it to say that we need to approach the study of Christ's return with some humility. We can be certain that Christ will return, but we need to exercise caution when we talk about how and when. This leads to the final point.

The real question about Christ's return is not, "When will it happen?" but, "Am I ready?" We do not know when Christ will return, nor do we know how long we have to live. None of us are promised tomorrow. But we do know this - we can be ready. As the writer of Hebrews states:

Just as people are destined to die once, and after that to face judgment, so Christ was sacrificed once to take away the sins of many; and he will appear a second time, not to bear sin, but to bring salvation to those who are waiting for him.

You can be among those to whom Christ brings salvation. Are you? I realize that I keep asking the question, but this is The Question. Are you ready to meet God?

Ten: What Now?

What if I made a decision to step over the line? Then what? What is expected of me? What should I do now?

The decision to follow Christ is a starting point, not an ending one. If you have decided to follow Jesus you need to take some next steps. And while everyone's spiritual journey is unique, there are a handful of practices everyone should adopt. Let me share five.

Worship: You need to reshape your world in ways that reflect his glory not your own. This will require a lot more from you than simply attending "worship services," but it starts there. Join a good church and become involved. This is the vehicle that God designed to advance his Kingdom in your life and around the world. Since shortly after the resurrection Christians have been meeting to pray, sing, hear the Word of God preached and participate in the sacraments of baptism and communion. Don't put this off. It's a necessary first step.

Connect: We were made in the image of a Triune God. Among the many things this implies is that we need each other. Attending worship services is a start, but it's too easy to be lost in the crowd. You need to be known. You need to be loved, cared for, encouraged and held accountable by people who love God and know what is going on in your life. One of the easiest ways to move in this direction is by joining together with a few others for weekly times of Bible study, prayer and fellowship. Be intentional about building this into your life. Christianity is not a solo sport.

Grow: Many people make a decision for Christ and then stall. This is never the plan. Each day we should grow closer to God. Part of the way we do this is by making certain spiritual exercises a regular part of our day. Prayer and Bible reading are at the very top of that list. I recommend that you set aside twenty minutes a day for this – ten to read and ten to pray. The first thing in the morning is ideal, but any time works. There are other spiritual disciplines to embrace, such as fasting, service, solitude, et al., but daily Bible reading and prayer are essential to your spiritual wellbeing. Start here. Serve: In his letter to the Ephesians, Paul tells us that we are "God's handiwork, created in Christ Jesus to do good works, which God prepared in advance for us to do." In his letter to the Corinthians he explains that every one of us has been supernaturally equipped to serve others. You need to serve. Find ways to help others. There are lots of formal and informal ways to do this. Just know this: you cannot grow past a certain point in your relationship with God unless you are serving others.

Serve: In his letter to the Ephesians, Paul tells us that we are "God's handiwork, created in Christ Jesus to do good works, which God prepared in advance for us to do." In his letter to the Corinthians he explains that every one of us has been supernaturally equipped to serve others. You need to serve. Find ways to help others. There are lots of formal and informal ways to do this. Just know this: you cannot grow past a certain point in your relationship with God unless you are serving others.

Share: The last area where we need to take action requires boldness and an open hand. Everything we own belongs to God, and we are expected to be good stewards of it all; that includes both our faith and our finances. To be as direct as I can be, you need to tell others about Jesus Christ. They need to hear about his life, death and resurrection. They need to hear that he offers them the free gift of eternal life and to hear about the changes he has made in your life. You need to invite them to church or some other Christian meeting. You also need to freely share your money. Your first gifts should go back to God (i.e., the church). You also need to share with the poor.

I hope you take these next steps. Jesus meets us wherever we are, but his plan is never to leave us there. It's time to grow. And that is a wonderful thing, because spiritual growth is its own reward. The more you become like Jesus, the better life becomes. Don't put this off.

ENDNOTES

[1] When theologians refer to "the work of Christ" they are referring to what he accomplished by dying on the cross.

[2] Luke 14:26

[3] Some have tried to reduce the Christian faith to "Love God and Love Others." (William Booth, founder of the Salvation Army, once sent out a telegram simply reading "Others.") Far too much truth is left out for either of these tag lines to represent the Christian faith, but they do point us in the right direction.

[4] Matthew 22:36-40.

[5] Romans 10:14

[6] Christ had a four-fold critique of first-century Judaism. 1) He argued that they misunderstood the size of their problem. The Jews knew that sin created a barrier between them and God, but they thought it was one they could bridge. Jesus said they were wrong. He taught that God was much holier than they imagined and that sin was more destructive than they feared. 2) He argued that they misunderstood the ultimate purpose of the Law. Jesus loved and affirmed the Law. In fact, he not only said that he had come to fulfill it, he also claimed that it was true down to the smallest detail. But his understanding of "the rules" differed from that of his fellow rabbis in two ways. First, he interpreted the Law differently than they did. (The Sermon on the Mount makes it clear that Jesus was teaching that we need to keep it in thought as well as in practice. This changed everything. It meant that everyone failed.) Secondly, Jesus argued that God gave them the Law to make this very point! He agreed that it had other purposes, but taught that if they would stop rationalizing their poor behavior long enough to actually study it, they would realize how much trouble they were in (see Mt. 5:20). The Law was like an answer key that not only made it clear that everyone was failing the test, but that we could never be good enough to earn God's favor. 3) He argued that they misunderstood what God was trying to do. The Jews could not imagine anything greater than the glory days of King David, therefore they longed for a Messiah who would overthrow the Romans and return Israel to power. Jesus dismissed these hopes as way too small. He claimed that his Father intended to bring every square inch of the universe back into his kingdom; consequently Jesus had been sent to defeat evil, begin reclaiming control and extending peace and justice to all God's children, not just the Jews. 4) Finally, he argued that they misunderstood the role of the Messiah. Given that the Jews misunderstood the nature of the kingdom, it follows that they misunderstood the nature of the king. They wanted a political and military leader. Jesus had come as

the Savior of the World. In these ways and more, Jesus disrupted the lives, power and prestige of the other rabbis.

7 Modern Judaism is broken into three branches: the Orthodox, Conservative and Reformed. Within each of those divisions, some people are more engaged in their faith than others. It's impossible to speak about what "the Jews" know or do not know about the Messianic prophecies. My experience is that most of the Jews I talk to are not familiar with them at all. Some are aware of them but understand them quite differently than I have presented in this study.

8 Mosheh ben Maimon, a preeminent medieval Jewish philosopher whose writings on Jewish law and ethics are a cornerstone of Jewish scholarship and whose fourteen-volume Mishneh Torah carries canonical authority, was very clear in stating that the Messiah had not yet come. For many Jews, this is a definitive word against Jesus. To embrace him as Savior and Lord would be an act of gross disrespect to their family and faith.

9 The entire Bible makes the claim that there is only one God and one way to approach him – i.e., through Christ. If we look back to the Old Testament we find: 1) so many warnings against worshipping anyone or anything other than the one true God that some scholars claim it is the most frequent topic in the Bible; 2) specific instructions to avoid the polytheistic views of the people around them. We find the same thing in the New Testament- e.g., in the sermons preached after the resurrection the apostles announce, "...there is no other name under heaven through which men can be saved." (Acts 4:12)

10 Two metaphors are commonly employed here: 1) Different religions are simply different roads up the same mountain. People might call God by different names but are praying to the same entity. We will meet at the top; 2) Like blind men touching different parts of the same elephant, different religions emphasize different aspects of the same thing.

11 Confucius says, "Don't do to others what you do not want them to do to you." Jesus says, "Do unto others as you would have them do unto you." These are different, but similar. We could come up with other examples.
12 In an essay entitled, "Isn't One Religion As Good As Another?" J.I. Packer writes, "The more one thinks about the question, the odder it seems. 'Good for what?' The great religions do not even claim to be good for the same thing." J.I. Packer, Isn't One Religion As Good As Another?, Hard Questions, Frank Colquhoun, ed. IVP, 1976, p. 15.

13 Advocates of the idea that all religions are the same often reduce every view down to the idea –first framed in the nineteenth century – that the essence of religion is, "The Fatherhood of God and the brotherhood of man." But this approach both ignores critical distinctions and summarizes

faiths in ways that makes them virtually unrecognizable to their adherents. Using this same approach we could say to parents, "You dropped a child off in the nursery, we will be sure you get a child back. It may not be the exact same child. But, hey, a child is a child is a child. They are all essentially the same."

[14] Some today actually assemble their own religion, mixing a little bit of reincarnation with a bit of Taoism, sprinkled with both Jesus and Yoga. Often the component parts are mutually contradictory.

[15] It's worth noting that sincerity is not a test of truth – i.e., you can sincerely believe that $1 + 1 = 5$ and your sincerity does not change the fact that you are wrong. It is also worth noting that acting like everything is true is not a loving thing to do. If someone asked you for directions to the hospital you would be unlikely to say, "All roads lead there; take whatever road you like best." Instead you would give him specific directions. If there really is only one way to the hospital – or heaven – then those who suggest that any road will get you there are not being open-minded and helpful. They are being dangerous.

[16] In arguing that there is one way that is true, I am not suggesting that we should be intolerant of other views, either personally or nationally. One of the great things about America is that we provide legal protection for different religious beliefs. (The U.S. has no national, state-sponsored faith or church such as they have in much of Europe.) This is a good thing. We should protect the religious freedoms of others and be charitable with those with whom we disagree because the Christian faith cannot be forced on anyone, and all we need is a free marketplace of ideas to do our work. However, it is one thing to be charitable and it is quite another to suggest that other views are true. It is one thing to make sure people can follow the dictates of their conscience without fear of persecution – i.e. that religions enjoy equal protection under the law – and quite another to suggest that all religions are equal or equally valid. People have equal value, but ideas do not, nor do cultures.

[17] R.C. Sproul writes: The issue of Matthew rests not on the issue of parthenogenesis (virgin birth) but on the issue of genesis itself. Creation is the unique event to beat all unique events. It's not so amazing that a God who has the power to bring the universe into being from nothing (ex nihilo) – without preexistent matter to work with, without means, but by the sheer omnipotent power of his voice – can also produce the birth of a baby by supernaturally fertilizing a material egg in a woman's womb.

[18] Some will argue that what is suggested here is similar to stories found in Greek legends, where there are many accounts of a divine "person" having sexual intercourse with a human (usually a god with a woman), but these arguments are not really relevant. The angel Gabriel spoke "with reverent

reserve" in stating that the Holy Spirit will "overshadow" her. There is not a claim to sexual relations. Rather, the claim is that Mary was a virgin – and a virgin conception (the claim is not of a virgin birth but a virgin conception) is unique. (The Tyndale Commentary on Luke, Leon Morris, 1974, p. 71-73).

[19] I am quoting Genesis 3:14 from the New American Standard Version (NASV) because it makes the point more clearly than the New International Version. Translation work involves thousands of decisions and compromises. A more literal translation – which is the NASV – is often clunky and more difficult to understand. But when translators make things more readable fine points are sometimes lost. The Hebrew term for "seed," is zera. This term is seldom used today, so I understand the decision of the NIV translators to use "offspring" – but a key point is lost when they do.

[20] We are not expected to understand all of this from Genesis 3 alone. Like many of the Old Testament prophecies, it only becomes clear later on. However, once we read Genesis 3 in light of the life of Christ we understand what was being implied. The idea of a virgin birth was introduced thousands of years before it occurred.

[21] Some have argued that the word that is used here for virgin (almah) has been mistranslated – that is, it should read "young woman" instead. They are wrong. While it is true that almah can be translated "young woman," it is usually not. In fact, of the eight times it is used in the Old Testament, it is only used that way once. More importantly, that particular definition does not work here. Think about it. Isaiah steps up on his soap box to make an important prediction. In his role as a prophet he announces that God has given them a way to recognize the Messiah. "You will be able to tell when God's anointed arrives because (insert drum roll here) he will be born to a....young woman!" Hmm, how exactly does that narrow things down? The correct translation of almah in Isaiah 7 is the most common one: virgin. For the record, this is certainly how Christ's contemporaries understood this passage. The Hebrew Bible they read – a Greek translation called the Septuagint, which was translated into Greek about 200 B.C. – translated the Hebrew term almah with the Greek term parthenos, which clearly means virgin.

[22] Luke is not only a physician, he is also an historian. In the latter capacity he is known for making very detailed reports. Where other New Testament writers mention "a withered hand" (Mark 3:1), Luke says that the man's "right hand was withered" (Luke 6:6, emphasis mine). When another writer reports that someone had "a fever" (Mt 8:14), Luke diagnosed it as a "high fever" (Luke 4:38, emphasis mine). As Blanchard has noted, "he would hardly have invented a story that would contradict his medical knowledge and make him the laughing stock of his fellow physicians." (Blanchard, p. 9).

156

[23] Christ was (is) able to save us because he avoided the sin of Adam that the rest of us inherit from our parents; therefore he had a chance to live a perfect life – which he in fact did. Christ faced all of the same temptations Adam did and withstood them. Had Jesus been born as a normal man he would not have been able to live a perfect life. God by-passed the inherited sin nature of the human race by supernaturally placing His Son in the womb of a virgin. The Virgin Birth is nothing to wink at or be casual about; the entire Gospel rests on it.

[24] I came across this illustration in Michael Green's chapter, Skepticism in the Church, in The Truth of God Incarnate, Hodder and Stoughton: London, 1977.

[25] Those who deny the Virgin Birth are left to explain who Christ's father was and why anyone would hold Mary in very high regard.

[26] The term canon comes from a Greek term meaning "rule" or "measuring stick." It is used to refer to the list of books that are considered to have authority. The New Testament canon refers to the 27 books that begin with Matthew's Gospel and end with The Revelation of Jesus Christ to John.

[27] Hebrews 1:3

[28] For a more complete explanation of revelation and the Bible, see FencePosts One, chapters 2 and 3.

[29] At the end of Colossians, we see Paul encouraging the believers there to forward his letter to others. Col 4:16 reads, "After this letter has been read to you, see that it is also read in the church of the Laodiceans and that you in turn read the letter from Laodicea." We also have evidence of this happening from extra-biblical sources, such as the writings of Justyn Martyr, a second century apologist. He describes a church service by saying: "On the day called the Day of the Sun all who live in cities or in the country gather together in one place, and the memoirs of the apostles or the writings of the prophets are read, as long as time permits; then, when the reader has ceased, the president verbally instructs, and exhorts to the imitation of these good things. Then we all rise together and pray."

[30] Two other gospels were mentioned in a favorable light in the early church prior to the formation of the canon. The first is the Gospel of the Hebrews, which has never been found. The second is the Gospel of Thomas, which is a compilation of sayings of Jesus rather than an account of His ministry. The other gospels were written later – often one hundred or more years later. Many of them are Gnostic in origin and do not conform to the teachings of Christ as recorded by Matthew, Mark, Luke and John.

[31] Epicurus, quoted in Lee Strobel, Case for Faith, p. 25.

[32] The Book of Job engages this topic most directly. In it Job asks God "why" he was allowing so many things to go wrong. In fact, Job attempts to put God in the dock and force him to justify his actions. In the end, much of what is going on remains a mystery to Job. Not only are the explanations his friends give him wrong, but when God does come down to meet with him it is not to justify his actions, it is to remind Job that God is God. Thankfully, that proves to be enough for Job. He does not get all of his questions answered, but He does get God's presence.

[33] Certain toy dolls are programmed to say "I love you." Do these dolls really love the little girls who are playing with them? Of course not. To experience love that doll would need to be able to choose to love or not to love. Real love involves a choice.

[34] In Romans 8:22 we are told that all creation has been affected by our sin. I am indebted to David Bentley Hart for the phrase, "the long melancholy aftermath of a primordial catastrophe."

[35] In John 16:33 Jesus said, "You will have suffering in this world."

[36] Matthew 11:19

[37] The only thing approaching a physical description of Jesus is found in Isaiah 53.

[38] In The Reason for God, Timothy Keller attempts to explain the trauma experienced by Christ on the cross by noting that the agony we experience at the loss of a relationship is among the worst imaginable. He first discusses how unpleasant any criticism and condemnation is before then noting that the rejection of a spouse or parent is exponentially worse. Finally, he explains that God the Son had enjoyed the perfect favor and infinite love of the Father from eternity past, but on the cross that was lost. (Timothy Keller, The Reason for God. New York: Riverhead Books, 2008, p. 29.

[39] John 10:18

[40] Those who advanced the Post-Mill view believed that as the Gospel spread and the church grew, society would get better and better. Since this has not happened – and since the twentieth century was the bloodiest on record – this view has lost favor.

BIOGRAPHY

Mike Woodruff is the senior pastor of Christ Church, a growing, community church with campuses in both Lake Forest and Highland Park, IL. In addition to founding The Ivy Jungle Network and serving as the President of Scholar Leaders International, Mike has worked as both a college minister and management consultant. As an author he has published over two hundred articles for business and ministry publications and edited or contributed to several books.   He holds degrees from DePauw University and Trinity Evangelical Divinity School and has an honorary Doctorate of Divinity from Sterling College. Mike and his wife Sheri have three sons, Austin, Benjamin and Jason.